Diet recommendations during bladder cancer

Diet can support the affected organs and is not a treatment for the disease. Please check these recommendations always with a nutrition consultant, therapist, doctor or dietician. The recipes and the list of ingredients are supporting the conventional medical therapy.
The calorie disclosures of fresh ingredients (fruit and vegetables) vary according to quality and time of harvest. The contents were checked by a dietician and a nutrition consultant for the Traditional Chinese Medicine (TCM).

Author:
©2017 Josef Miligui
www.ebns.at

AF206284

Source:
The lists are created from the EBNS database for nutritional counseling. The database is used by dietitians, therapists and doctors for advising the patient / client.

Literature:
The specialist literature and the training documents of the German and Austrian dietary and traditional Chinese medicine serve as a knowledge base. We have used the documents as a basis of knowledge, adapted it to our experience and completed them.
http://di-book.com

Title Photo:
©2008 Erika Weixlbaumer

Production and publishing:
BoD – Books on Demand, Norderstedt
ISBN: 9783746097787

Diet recommendations during bladder cancer

1 Treatment strategy

Contaminants and irritants excreted via the bladder should be avoided. Risk factors such as smoking and extreme coffee consumption must be eliminated.

Bearberry leaves have a germ-inhibiting effect, cranberry juice reduces the colonization of bacteria in the bladder.

Broccoli, kale, cauliflower and Brussels sprouts
Radish
Sour milk products
Bearberry leaf
Cranberry juice / cranberry
Bladder / Kidney teas

2 Avoid

Smoking, coffee, coke, alcohol, spicy food, black tea, sugar, large quantities of sour fruit juices

3 Breakfast
kkal. per serving

4 Snack

5 Lunch

6 Afternoon

7 Dinner

8   Any time

9 Recipes

(recommendable) = You can use more.
(little) = You should use less than specified or omit.

9.1 8 treasures of rice

Diuretic, warming the body from the inside, expands blood vessels, strengthens the muscles, regulates internal organs functions, promotes spleen, calms nerves.
Cooking time approx. 1 hour
Calories p. portion: 212
4 portions
Allergens:

Quantity of ingredients:
Lily bulbs 1 table spoon / 5g. (recommended)
Longane 1 table spoon / 5g. (yes)
King Solomon's-seal 1 table spoon / 5g. (yes)
Yam root, yam root tuber 1 table spoon / 5g. (yes)
Coix (seeds) YiYi Ren 1 table spoon / 5g. (yes)
Rice wild (nature rice) 1 1/2 cups / 240g. (recommended)
Water 8-10 cups / 800g. (yes)

Cooking instructions:
Each one 1 tbsp: Bai He, Longan, Yu Zhu, Da Zao, Shan Yao, Lian Mi, Yi Yi Ren, Qian Shi
Add hot water and soak for about 30 minutes. Then add 1 - 2 cups of rice (normal) and simmer for 1/2 to 1 hour until the rice is very soft. Or: Cook for about 3 hours with the herbs a congee. Then the herbs do not have to be soaked.

9.2 Adzuki Bean and Rice Soup

Strengthens spleen, heart, kidney and stomach, supports urination, improves blood circulation, reduces inflammation.
Cooking time approx. 2 hours
Calories p. portion: 199
1 portions
Allergens:

Quantity of ingredients:
Adzuki beans 8 table spoons / 40g. (yes)
Rice round grain 2 table spoons / 20g. (yes)
Water 1 1/2 cups / 200g. (yes)
Honey 1 table spoon / 8g. (little)

Cooking instructions:
Boil soaked adzuki beans and round grain rice in a ratio of 4: 1 in water until a thin pulp has formed. Sweet as needed; possibly puree.
Effect: This recipe strengthens kidney, spleen and stomach and is particularly suitable for mothers with too little milk flow.

9.3   Antipasti

Improves blood circulation, anti-inflammatory, relieves pain. Diuretic, promotes digestion, reduces blood pressure. antioxidativ, antibacterial, affects anorexia, improves digestion, stomach weakness, stimulating.
Cooking time approx. 40 min
Calories p. portion: 100
3 portions
Allergens:

Quantity of ingredients:
Pepperoni 1 piece / 5g. (yes)
Lemon juice 1 table spoon / 10g. (little)
Aubergine 1 piece / 300g. (yes)
Tomato 4 pieces / 200g. (recommended)
Zucchini 5/8 oz / 200g. (recommended)
Lemon peel 1/2 piece / 3g. (yes)
Olive oil 1 table spoon / 15g. (yes)
Basil (fresh) 8 leaves / 5g. (yes)
Salt 1 pinch / 0,5g. (little)
Coriander 1/2 teaspoon / 2g. (yes)

Cooking instructions:
Preheat the oven to 250 degrees Celsius and bake the hot peppers until the bowl becomes dark (about 20 minutes). Cover the hot peppers with a clear film and allow to cool. Peel the skin and cut into strips about 2 cm wide. Cut tomatoes in half and spread with oil in slices of aubergine and bake in the oven at 200 degrees golden brown (about 10 minutes) Fry the zucchini slices in the grill pan (without fat). Mix everything together, mix the marinade of olive oil, salt and lemon peel and pour over the vegetables, sprinkle with coriander. Leave for 1 hour.

9.4 Apricot Oat Balls with Acai powder

Strengthens immune system, little laxative, antioxidativ.
Cooking time approx. 20 min
Calories p. portion: 768
2 portions
Allergens: AHO

Quantity of ingredients:
Oat flakes (whole grain) 1/4 lbs - 4oz / 125g. (recommended)
Apricot dried 1/4 lbs - 4oz / 125g. (little)
Almond 1/4 lbs - 4oz / 100g. (yes)
Honey 2 table spoons / 14g. (little)
Acai powder 3 teaspoons / 9g. (recommended)
Lemon juice 2 table spoons / 9g. (little)

Cooking instructions:
Lightly chop the sliced almonds in the pan and let them cool. Then pour the apricots in the blender and add lemon juice. Mix all the ingredients together. If the mass is too loose add some honey. Finally, form small balls and roll them in oat flakes.

9.5 Baked chicory

Mineral supporter and is full of A-B-C vitamins.
Cooking time approx. 20 min
Calories p. portion: 230
2 portions
Allergens: AG

Quantity of ingredients:
Chicory 4 pieces / 500g. (recommended)
Cream, sweet 30% 2 table spoons / 40g. (little)
Breadcrumbs (wheat bread, bread roll) 2 table spoons / 20g. (yes)
Rice Basmati 1/2 cup / 60g. (yes)
Water 3 cups / 300g. (yes)
Salt 1 pinch / 1g. (little)

Cooking instructions:
Blanch chicory in hot water whole for about 5 minutes; place in a casserole dish; put some sweet cream over it; put the bread crumbs over the chicory and gratinate. Place the rice in salted water, heat till it boils and let it simmer over low heat for about 15 minutes.

9.6 Basic recipe for a beef broth (clear)

Strengthens muscles, tendons and bones, reduces blood pressure, strengthens immune system, prevents cancer, reduces radiation damage, stimulates digestion, reduces pain, promotes digestion, diuretic. Rosemary stimulates digestion.
Cooking time approx. 4-8 hours
Calories p. portion: 114
10 portions
Allergens: O

Quantity of ingredients:
Beef soup meat 1,1 lbs / 500g. (yes)
Beef meatbones 5/8 oz / 200g. (yes)
Vinegar (Red wine vinegar) 1 dash / 3g. (yes)
Juniper berry 8 pieces / 6g. (recommended)
Rosemary 1 pinch / 1g. (yes)
Carrot 3 pieces / 210g. (recommended)
Parsnip 2 pieces / 300g. (yes)
Leek 1 piece / 200g. (yes)
Ginger fresh 1/2 teaspoon / 5g. (yes)
Lovage 1 stem / 15g. (yes)
Clove 2 pieces / 2g. (yes)
Pimento 6 pieces / 12g. (yes)
Anise (Common Fennel) 2 pieces / 1g. (yes)
Salt 1 teaspoon / 5g. (little)
Water 3,3 lbs / 1300g. (yes)

Cooking instructions:
Heat water, a dash of red wine vinegar, some juniper berries, a little rosemary, bones and meat till it boils; add carrot, parsnip, leek, ginger, lovage, clove, allspice, star anise and a little salt; simmer for 4-8 hours then strain.
Refrigerate for later use.

9.7 Basic recipe for a chicken broth worming

Strengthens blood, strengthens bone marrow, reduces blood pressure, strengthens immune system, prevents cancer, reduces radiation damage, promotes sweating, dissolves stagnation, good to fight loss of appetite, flatulence.
Cooking time approx. 2-3 hours
Calories p. portion: 90
9 portions
Allergens: L

Quantity of ingredients:
Chicken meat 1/2 piece / 600g. (yes)
Carrot 2 pieces / 150g. (recommended)
Leek 1 stick / 45g. (yes)
Celery root 1 piece / 500g. (recommended)
Ginger fresh 2 slices / 2g. (yes)
Fenugreek (Trigonella foenum-graecum) 1 teaspoon / 2g. (yes)
Juniper berry 1 teaspoon / 3g. (recommended)
Bay leaf 3 pieces / 2g. (yes)
Water 4 cup / 900g. (yes)

Cooking instructions:
Remove chicken parts from fat. Place chicken pieces in a saucepan with hot water and heat till it boils briefly, skimming any resulting foam. Add coarsely chopped vegetables and all spices and cook over medium heat for 2 to 3 hours. Strain the finished soup. Throw away vegetables and bones.
Tip: If you want to use the meat as a soup insert, take out after 45 minutes and return only the bones in the soup.
Refrigerate for later use.

9.8 Basic recipe for a duck broth

Forcing spleen, strengthens blood, supports urination, reduces blood pressure, strengthens immune system, prevents cancer, reduces radiation damage.
Cooking time approx. 2-3 hours
Calories p. portion: 61
6 portions
Allergens: L

Quantity of ingredients:
Water 2 cup / 450g. (yes)
Duck (heart) 5/8 oz / 200g. (yes)
Duck (slaughtered) 1/4 lbs - 4oz / 100g. (yes)
Carrot 2 pieces / 100g. (recommended)
Celery root 1/2 piece / 600g. (recommended)

Cooking instructions:
Cook duck pieces with vegetables for 2-3 hours. Sift broth through a fine sieve and refrigerate for later use.

The innards can be reused: You cut them finely and leaves them for a few minutes with fresh vegetables in the broth draw. Sprinkle with parsley before serving.

9.9 Basic recipe for a vegetable soup, nutritious

Reduces blood pressure, strengthens immune system, prevents cancer, forcing spleen, dissolves stagnation, promotes weight loss. Good to fight immunodeficiency, high blood pressure, depressions, diabetes, diarrhea, reduces blood lipids.
Cooking time approx. 2-3 hours
Calories p. portion: 48
5 portions
Allergens: L

Quantity of ingredients:
Olive oil 1 table spoon / 4g. (yes)
Onion white 1 piece / 60g. (yes)
Carrot 3 pieces / 200g. (recommended)
Parsnip 3/8 lbs - 6oz / 150g. (yes)
Celery root 1 cup / 100g. (recommended)
Ginger fresh 1/2 teaspoon / 2g. (yes)
Lemon 1/2 piece / 25g. (little)
Juniper berry 6 pieces / 6g. (recommended)
Thyme dried 1 pinch / 1g. (yes)
Lovage 1 table spoon / 3g. (yes)
Bay leaf 2 leaves / 1g. (yes)
Salt 1 pinch / 1g. (little)
Water 3 cups / 650g. (yes)

Cooking instructions:
Cut the vegetables into cubes.
Heat oil in hot pot, fry shortly onions and vegetables.
Add cold water, then add ginger, bay leaf and lemon juice.
Season with juniper, thyme and lovage. Cover for 2 - 3 hours on a low heat and simmer.
The used vegetables should be thrown away.
The basic recipe serves as a soup base and to refine vegetables, legumes or cereals.
If you want to eat vegetable soup immediately, add the desired vegetables half an hour before.
Refrigerate for later use.

9.10 Basmati rice + Zucchini tofu dish

Diuretic, supports urination, harmonizes spleen and stomach, reduces flatulence, good to fight body overweight and high blood pressure.
Antioxidativ, promotes digestion, perspiration, reduces blood lipids, forcing spleen.
Cooking time approx. 20 min
Calories p. portion: 146
4 portions
Allergens: E

Quantity of ingredients:
Soy Tofu 5/8 lbs - 8oz / 250g. (yes)
Olive oil 2 table spoons / 6g. (yes)
Coriander 1/2 teaspoon / 4g. (yes)
Ginger fresh 1/2 teaspoon / 4g. (yes)
Rice Basmati 1/2 cup / 60g. (yes)
Water 3 cups / 200g. (yes)
Zucchini 1 piece / 700g. (recommended)

Cooking instructions:
Cut tofu cubes and marinate with olive oil, tamari, crushed coriander and ginger. Leave at least 1 hour.
Cook Basmati rice with the water. You can season with onion and cardamom.
Roast zucchini and tofu in pan in the hot oil for approx. 5-7 min.
Serve rice and tofu on a plate.
Add the parsley.
Can also be used as a salad for the home and on the go.

9.11 Beef broth

Warming and nourishing, forces.
Cooking time approx. 2-6 hours
Calories p. portion: 125
7 portions
Allergens: L

Quantity of ingredients:
Water 4 cup / 1000g. (yes)
Lemon 2 daches / 2g. (little)
Beef meat 1,1 lbs / 500g. (yes)
Beef meatbones 2 pieces / 0g. (yes)
Turmeric (yellow root) 1 pinch / 1g. (recommended)
Carrot 2 pieces / 100g. (recommended)
Celery root 1 inch / 25g. (recommended)
Parsley root 1 piece / 150g. (yes)
Onion white 1 piece / 50g. (yes)
Bay leaf 2-3 leaves / 2g. (yes)
Coriander 1/2 teaspoon / 2g. (yes)
Ginger fresh 1 inch / 2g. (yes)
Wakame 1 inch / 1g. (yes)
Parsley 1 stem / 10g. (yes)

Cooking instructions:
In a saucepan with water (enough to cover the meat), add a few drops
of lemon juice, a little turmeric, beef and bones, heat till it boils and
simmer for a while; then pour away the whole broth, clean the pot, rinse
off meat and bones with hot water (this will save you from foaming) and
put it back to the saucepan with hot water (amount as you like); add a
good pinch of turmeric, carrot, celery, parsley root to the pot; add onion,
bay leaves, coriander, a piece of sliced ginger, a strip of wakame, a
stalk of parsley; boil everything together and simmer for 2-6 hours (if the
meat is to be used otherwise, take it out of the broth after 1 1/2 - 2
hours, as soon as it is cooked, the bones are returned to the broth);
When the cooking time is over, pour the broth through a sieve and
discard all ingredients.

Notes: The longer the broth has cooked, the warmer but more
nourishing it is. It is after cooling for 3-4 days in the refrigerator durable.
The broth can be drunk hot or used as a base for soups with cereals,
potatoes and fresh vegetables.

9.12 Beetroot soup

Strengthens gastrointestinal function, expands blood vessels, strengthens the muscles, antioxidativ. Promotes digestion, dissolves stagnation.
Cooking time approx. 20-30 min
Calories p. portion: 282
4 portions
Allergens: G

Quantity of ingredients:
Olive oil 2 table spoons / 20g. (yes)
Onion white 1 piece chopped / 50g. (yes)
Garlic 1 clove / 2g. (yes)
Red beet 2,2 lbs (Peeled and diced) / 1000g. (recommended)
Cumin (Caraway seed) 1 table spoon / 7g. (yes)
Curcuma 1 teaspoon / 2g. (yes)
Oregano fresh 1 pinch of fresh / 2g. (yes)
Peppers (rose peppers) 1 teaspoon / 2g. (yes)
Créme fraiche cheese 1/4 lbs - 4oz / 125g. (yes)

Cooking instructions:
Heat the oil in a saucepan, fry the onions and garlic in dark brown. Add cumin, turmeric, oregano and salt and deglaze with 1 liter of water. Cook the beetroot for about 20 minutes. Puree the soup and serve in soup bowls with 1 tbsp. crème fraiche. Finally, sprinkle the rose pepper over it.

9.13 Bircher-muesli with yogurt, nuts and apple

Fibre-rich, relieves constipation, strengthens immune system, forcing spleen, promotes weight loss. Good to fight immunodeficiency, loss of appetite.
Cooking time approx. 2 hours and more
Calories p. portion: 383
1 portions
Allergens: AGH

Quantity of ingredients:
Muesli 2 table spoons / 20g. (recommended)
Oat flakes (whole grain) 2 table spoons / 20g. (recommended)
Yogurt (natural, 3.5% fat) 6 table spoons / 80g. (yes)
Lemon 1 table spoon / 10g. (little)
Acerola fruit nectar or powder 1/2 teaspoon / 1g. (little)
Apple (sour) 1 piece / 170g. (little)
Hazelnuts 1 table spoon / 10g. (yes)

Cooking instructions:
Soak oatmeal in the yogurt for several hours in the fridge. Add rubbed nuts, lemon juice, acerola, grated apple. For sweets, raisins can be used.

9.14 Carp soup

Increase milk production and sweating, dissolves stagnation, reduces blood pressure, strengthens immune system, improves blood circulation, improves medication effect, stimulates appetite. Strengthens gastrointestinal function, expands blood vessels.
Cooking time approx. 2 hours
Calories p. portion: 499
2 portions
Allergens: DO

Quantity of ingredients:
Carp 1,1 lbs / 500g. (yes)
Salt 1 pinch / 1g. (little)
Vinegar (Apple vinegar) 1 teaspoon / 3g. (yes)
Thyme 1 Twig / 3g. (yes)
Juniper berry 8 pieces / 3g. (recommended)
Carrot 2 pieces / 200g. (recommended)
Leek 1 piece / 200g. (yes)
Onion white 1 piece / 60g. (yes)
Ginger fresh 1/2 teaspoon / 2g. (yes)
Bay leaf 3 leaves / 1g. (yes)
White wine 1/2 cup / 125g. (little)
Basil 3 leaves / 1g. (yes)

Cooking instructions:
Preparation: When shopping at the fishmonger, remove the fillets from a medium-sized, whole carp and also pack the fish head, spine with bones and tail.

Cut the fillets into 1 cm cubes; salt and set aside.

Place fish head, backbone and tail of carp in plenty of cold water; heat till it boils and scoop the foam; add a dash of vinegar, a fresh sprig of thyme, juniper berries; Add carrot, a piece of leek and chopped onion; add a thick slice of ginger, some peppercorns, 1 bay leaf, salt; simmer for about 1 1/2 hours and pour the stock through a sieve.

Put the carp pieces in a saucepan; pour a shot of white wine; Add rose paprika, basil leaves, finely ground carrots, dried thyme and the stock and warm; Boil the ingredients for about 5 minutes until the fish pieces are cooked.
Variants: Thicken the soup with kudzu or mashed potatoes.
This fits: baguette and dry white wine.

9.15 Celery juice

Mineral and vitamin rich, forces metabolism and dehydrating effect.
Cooking time approx. 5 min
Calories p. portion: 33
1 portions
Allergens: L

Quantity of ingredients:
Celery root 1/2 piece / 200g. (recommended)
Water 1 cup / 120g. (yes)
Salt 1 pinch / 0,5g. (little)

Cooking instructions:
Peel celeriac and cut into pieces and juice. Mix with water and salt as needed.

9.16 Cereal fruit pulp

Lots of vitamin C, strengthens immune system, antiparasitic.
Cooking time approx. 10 min
Calories p. portion: 175
1 portions
Allergens: A

Quantity of ingredients:
Oat flakes (whole grain) 1/2 oz / 20g. (recommended)
Water 3,5 oz / 90g. (yes)
Apple juice (natural cloudy) 1/4 lbs - 4oz / 100g. (yes)
Rapeseed oil 1/8 oz / 5g. (recommended)

Cooking instructions:
Heat the water till it boils the add the cereals. Instant flakes you only
need to mix with hot water. Stir fruit juice or puree and grease. The
fresh fruit (for example, apples, pears, peaches) can be raw or
kneaded. Frozen fruit or industrially produced fruit jars without added
sugar are also suitable. Bananas should be mixed with less sweet fruit.

9.17 Chicken with white turnips on rice

Strengthens bone marrow. Rice to drain the body at overweight and
high blood pressure.
Cooking time approx. 45 min
Calories p. portion: 324
4 portions
Allergens: GL

Quantity of ingredients:
Butter organic 2 table spoons / 20g. (yes)
Olive oil 2 table spoons / 20g. (yes)
Onion white 1 piece / 60g. (yes)
Turnips 4 pieces / 200g. (recommended)
Garlic 2 pieces / 3g. (yes)
Basic recipe for a chicken soup (warming) 1 cup / 100g. (yes)
Parsley 2 table spoons / 15g. (yes)
Salt 1 pinch / 1g. (little)
Olive oil 1 teaspoon / 4g. (yes)
Chicken meat 7/8 lbs / 400g. (yes)
Water 6 cups / 400g. (yes)
Rice Basmati 1 cup / 120g. (yes)

Cooking instructions:
In a heavy pot, heat the butter and the oil at low temperature. Add the
onion, stir and simmer for about 20 minutes on very low heat until soft
and golden brown. Add the chopped beets and the chopped garlic
cloves and stir well. Add the chicken broth or water, add some salt and
heat till it boils. Reduce the heat, put on the lid and simmer the beets for

about 20 minutes. Look in between if there is still enough liquid in the pot, and if necessary, pour in a few tablespoons of chicken stock. At the end there should be very little liquid in the pot. Remove the lid and allow the remaining liquid to evaporate, stirring constantly.

In the meantime roast the finely chopped chicken pieces in a frying pan with a little oil. Finally, sprinkle with a little chilli and fry for another minute while constantly turning.
Serve the pieces of chicken, turnips and rice on the plates, spread the sauce over them and sprinkle with parsley immediately.

Cook the rice in the ratio of 6 cups of water: 1 cup of rice.

Small, fresh, untreated beets do not need to be peeled. Otherwise, peel beets and place in hot water for 10 minutes. This makes them easier to digest and lose some of their sharp, pungent odor. White turnips are rich in vitamin C, potassium and folic acid.

9.18 Chickpeas with Raisins

Reduces blood pressure, strengthens immune system. Relaxes breast pressure, moisturizer dry skin, helps to fight incontinence. Strengthens spleen and stomach, strengthens the muscles.
Cooking time approx. 45 min
Calories p. portion: 429
2 portions
Allergens: EGO

Quantity of ingredients:
Chickpeas 1 cup / 120g. (yes)
Hijiki 1 table spoon / 7g. (yes)
Salt 1 pinch / 0,5g. (little)
Sunflower oil 1 table spoon / 10g. (yes)
Carrot 2 pieces / 160g. (recommended)
Raisins 2 table spoons / 18g. (yes)
Ginger fresh 1/2 teaspoon / 2g. (yes)
Cumin (Caraway seed) 1 pinch / 0,2g. (yes)
Lemon juice 1 dash / 1g. (little)
Sour cream 15% fat 1 table spoon / 8g. (recommended)
Curcuma 1 pinch / 0,2g. (yes)
Soybean milk 1 dash / 1g. (yes)
Coriander 1 pinch / 0,2g. (yes)
Soy sauce 1 dash / 1g. (yes)

Rice round grain 1/2 cup / 60g. (yes)
Water 3 cups / 250g. (yes)
Salt 1 pinch / 1g. (little)

Cooking instructions:
Preparation:
Soak chickpeas in cold water for several hours or overnight.

After that:
Pour soaking water away; put the chickpeas in cold water; Add 1 tbsp Hijiki and cook the chickpeas bite-proof; Add salt at the end of the cooking time.

Separately:
In a hot pan, fry oil, chopped carrots (more than chickpeas), raisins, grated ginger, plenty of cumin and salt until the carrots are half cooked; add the chickpeas and sea algae; Add lemon juice, a little sour cream, turmeric, soy or rice milk; a pinch of cilantro, add some soy sauce; Let it soak for a few minutes over low heat until the carrots are cooked.

Put the round grain rice with the water, salt and cook for about 20 minutes.

9.19 Clear soup from goose

Promotes sweating, dissolves stagnation. Reduces blood pressure, strengthens immune system, expands blood vessels, stimulates digestion, reduces pain.
Cooking time approx. 2-3 hours
Calories p. portion: 334
6 portions
Allergens:

Quantity of ingredients:
Goose parts 1,1 lbs / 500g. (yes)
Carrot 1 piece / 100g. (recommended)
Onion (shallot) 1 piece / 25g. (yes)
Leek 1 piece / 250g. (yes)
Parsley 1 Twig / 4g. (yes)
Lovage 1 Twig / 4g. (yes)
Chervil 1 pinch / 0,2g. (yes)
Water 4 cup / 1000g. (yes)
Salt 1 pinch / 0,5g. (little)

Cooking instructions:
Simmer goose pieces with vegetables and herbs for 2-3 hours. Sift through a fine cloth and cool. Degrease and store in the refrigerator.

9.20 Compote from apples

Apple (sweet) stops diarrhea, promotes digestion, appetizing, harmonizes the stomach. Warms stomach and spleen, improves blood circulation.
Cooking time approx. 10 min
Calories p. portion: 67
2 portions
Allergens:

Quantity of ingredients:
Apple (sweet) 1 piece / 220g. (recommended)
Water 1 1/2 cups / 220g. (yes)
Cinnamon ground 1 pinch / 1g. (yes)

Cooking instructions:
Cook the apples (organic) with the skin and seeds. Sprinkle with cinnamon.

9.21 Cottage cheese with steamed fruit

Good to fight loss of appetite, promotes digestion, supports urination.
Cooking time approx. 20 min
Calories p. portion: 214
2 portions
Allergens: G

Quantity of ingredients:
Cottage cheese 3/4 lbs / 300g. (yes)
Apple (sour) 1 piece / 100g. (little)
Pear 1 piece / 100g. (recommended)

Cooking instructions:
Wash apples and pears well, do not peel, and chop small. In a pot with steam filter, boil them al dente, remove and allow to cool down.
Serve the cheese, spread the fruit on it.

9.22 Couscous Salad

prevents cancer, forcing spleen, promotes digestion, stimulates liver function, reduces blood pressure, strengthens immune system, reduces radiation damage, diuretic.
Cooking time approx. 25 min
Calories p. portion: 338
3 portions
Allergens: A

Quantity of ingredients:
Water 1 cup / 100g. (yes)
Olive oil 1 table spoon / 15g. (yes)
Couscous 5/8 oz / 200g. (yes)
Lemon juice 2 table spoons / 30g. (little)
Lemon peel 1 teaspoon / 2g. (yes)
Tomato 2 pieces / 80g. (recommended)
Cucumber 1/4 lbs - 4oz / 100g. (recommended)
Carrot 1/4 lbs - 4oz / 100g. (recommended)
Parsley 1 Bunch / 100g. (yes)
Chives 1 Bunch / 100g. (yes)
Peppermint 3 twigs / 30g. (yes)

Cooking instructions:
Boil in a small saucepan 250 ml. water with salt and 1 tablespoon olive oil. Add the couscous, take the stove in the front and let it swell covered for 5 minutes. Put the couscous back on the stove and let it simmer for about 2 minutes with gentle stirring. If necessary, add 1 - 3 tbsp of hot water.
Mix the couscous with lemon juice, chopped lemon peel and 1 tbsp oil, season with salt and pepper and leave to set.
Add couscous with tomatoes, cucumber, parsley (all diced), carrots (grated), chives and mint (finely chopped). Season the couscous salad with lemon juice, salt and pepper.

9.23 Cranberry juice

Antibacterial, good to fight loss of appetite, arteriosclerosis, bladder infections, diarrhea, colds. Antipyretic, against free radicals, gout, diuretic, stomach ulcers, oral mucosa inflammation, rheumatism.
Cooking time approx. 5 min
Calories p. portion: 43
1 portions
Allergens:

Quantity of ingredients:
Cranberries 2 table spoons / 25g. (recommended)
Water 1 cup / 125g. (yes)
Honey 1 table spoon / 10g. (little)

Cooking instructions:
Mix the cranberries with a little water with the blender to a pulp. Add the remaining water and sweeten with the honey.

9.24 Cucumber salad

Diuretic, detoxifying, suppresses conversion of sugar into fat, lowers cholesterol, prevents cancer. Cucumber cools and moistens. Dill works against flatulence, anticonvulsant in gastrointestinal discomfort.
Cooking time approx. 5 min
Calories p. portion: 27
2 portions
Allergens: O

Quantity of ingredients:
Cucumber 1 piece / 400g. (recommended)
Salt 1 pinch / 1g. (little)
Dill 1 pinch / 1g. (yes)
Vinegar (Apple vinegar) 1 table spoon / 10g. (yes)

Cooking instructions:
Cut the cucumber (do not peel the BIO) thinly and season.

9.25 Delicately spiced zucchini with tomatoes

Diuretic, promotes digestion, helps to digest fat, reduces blood pressure, dissolves stagnation, antioxidativ, supports urination, diuretic, warming the body from the inside, expands blood vessels.
Cooking time approx. 10 min
Calories p. portion: 203
4 portions
Allergens:

Quantity of ingredients:
Olive oil 1 table spoon / 20g. (yes)
Onion white 2 pieces / 120g. (yes)
Zucchini 4 pieces / 800g. (recommended)
Oregano dried 1 pinch / 1g. (yes)
Basil (fresh) 6-8 leaves / 3g. (yes)
Salt 1 pinch / 1g. (little)
Tomato 2 pieces / 120g. (recommended)
Rice (whole grain) 1 cup / 120g. (recommended)
Water 6 cups / 400g. (yes)
Salt 1 pinch / 1g. (little)

Cooking instructions:
In a hot pan, fry olive oil, finely chopped onions and finely chopped zucchini until half cooked. Add plenty of dried oregano. Salt and chop the tomatoes for a few minutes until the zucchini are tender but crisp. Add fresh basil as desired.

Variation: Put some sheep's cheese over the tomatoes and finish cooking with the lid closed.

Place the rice in salted water, heat till it boils and let it simmer over low heat for about 15 minutes.

9.26 Fennel with roasted walnuts

Forcing spleen, detoxifying, reduces inflammation, improves blood circulation, improves medication effect, stimulates appetite, antioxidativ, promotes digestion, stimulates, dissolves stagnation.
Cooking time approx. 20 min
Calories p. portion: 342
4 portions
Allergens: HO

Quantity of ingredients:
Fennel 4 pieces / 800g. (recommended)
Nutmeg 1 pinch / 1g. (yes)
Ginger fresh 1/2 teaspoon / 1g. (yes)
Salt 1 pinch / 1g. (little)
White wine 1/2 cup / 125g. (little)
Peppers powder 1 pinch / 1g. (yes)
Olive oil 2 table spoons / 40g. (yes)
Walnuts 2 table spoons / 35g. (yes)

Water 1 1/2 cups / 220g. (yes)
Corn Grease (Polenta) 1 cup / 120g. (yes)
Salt 1 pinch / 1g. (little)

Cooking instructions:
Heat very little water in a pot; Fry the fennel in strips. Add Nutmeg, a
little grated ginger, add salt, a dash of white wine, rose paprika.
Simmer until the vegetables are cooked, but still crisp; stir in a little olive
oil; sprinkle with roasted walnuts.

Stir the polenta into a pot of hot water, stirring constantly, until the
polenta has the desired consistency. Salt.
Pull the polenta off the fire and let it swell for about 10 minutes.

9.27 Grated carrots with apple

Promotes spleen and liver, reduces blood pressure, strengthens
immune system, prevents cancer, reduces radiation damage, stops
diarrhea, promotes digestion, appetizing, harmonizes the stomach.
Cooking time approx. 10 min
Calories p. portion: 74
1 portions
Allergens:

Quantity of ingredients:
Carrot 1/4 lbs - 4oz / 100g. (recommended)
Apple (sweet) 1 piece / 50g. (recommended)
Lemon juice 2 teaspoons / 3g. (little)
Sugar substitute (sweetener) 1g. Or 0,034oz / 1g. (yes)

Cooking instructions:
Mix lemon juice with sweetener. Grate the washed, thinly peeled carrots
and the apple piece into the sauce and mix.

9.28 Grilled salmon steaks with cauliflower and
     potatoes

Improves digestion, regenerates skin, supports urination, lowers
cholesterol, supports digestion.
Cooking time approx. 30 min
Calories p. portion: 330
4 portions
Allergens: D

Quantity of ingredients:
Garlic 1 clove / 1g. (yes)
Onion (shallot) 1/2 piece / 5g. (yes)
Lemon juice 1 dach / 1g. (little)
Salt 1 pinch / 1g. (little)
Cauliflower 1 piece / 500g. (recommended)
Olive oil 2 table spoons / 20g. (yes)
Garlic 1 clove / 1g. (yes)
Water 2/3 cup / g. (yes)
Parsley 2 table spoons / 15g. (yes)
Potato 1,1 lbs / 500g. (yes)
Salt 1 pinch / 1g. (little)
Salmon 4 pieces (steaks) / 500g. (recommended)
Lemon 1/2 piece / 2g. (little)

Cooking instructions:
Garlic shallots mixture:
Finely squeeze the garlic, finely chop the shallots, add a dash of lemon juice and salt and stir. Mix with a little oil to a paste.

Cauliflower:
Cut the cauliflower into pieces.
Heat the oil in a heavy saucepan and fry the crushed garlic for a short time.
Add the cauliflower pieces and turn in the oil. Add a little water and cook until the cauliflower is firm. Strain the cauliflower and cook the remaining water until a thick sauce remains. Add the cauliflower and crush it roughly with a wooden spoon. Add the chopped parsley and salt.

Potatoes:
Cook the potato in a saucepan with plenty of water, strain and peel.

Salmon Steak:
Preheat the oven at about 180°C/356°F. Rub in the salmon slices with the garlic-scarlet mixture and grill as close as possible to the heat source for 4 to 8 minutes from both sides. You are done when the meat is easy to divide when you pierce with a fork.

Serve and sprinkle with lemon slices and the chopped parsley.

9.29 Grilled tofu with rice noodles, spinach and sugar snaps

Reduces flatulence. Supports urination, detoxifying. Good to fight blood circulation disorders. Strengthens gastrointestinal function, expands blood vessels, stimulates appetite. Promotes bowel movement, improves blood circulation.
Cooking time approx. 30 min
Calories p. portion: 327
4 portions
Allergens: E

Quantity of ingredients:
Sake 1/3 cup / 85g. (little)
Sugar cane sugar 1 table spoon / 7g. (little)
Garlic 5 cloves / 7g. (yes)
Onion (spring onion) 3 pieces / 60g. (yes)
Ginger fresh 1 inch / 5g. (yes)
Rapeseed oil 2 table spoons / 20g. (recommended)
Spinach 2 handful / 30g. (yes)
Peas, green 7/8 lbs / 400g. (yes)
Water 1 table spoon / g. (yes)
Rice noodles 1 package / 250g. (yes)
Water 4 cup / g. (yes)
Basil 1 table spoon / 3g. (yes)
Soy Tofu 1,1 lbs / 500g. (yes)

Cooking instructions:
In a medium bowl mix together: Tamari souce, rice wine, sugar, crushed garlic, spring onion, grated ginger, chopped basil and the rapeseed oil. Add the tofu and leave in the marinade for at least 1 hour. Cover the mangetout peas in a pan with a little water, lightly simmer 5 min. Add the spinach and steam again 3 min.

Cook the rice noodles according to manufacturer's instructions, drain, rinse again with warm water and drain.
Preheat the grill or oven grill, grill the tofu for 5 minutes on both sides and set aside.
Arrange the pasta on the plates, divide the vegetables all around and place the tofu over the noodles. Douse with the marinade.

9.30 Indian Dal soup

Strengthens heart and kidney, diuretic, calms the stomach, promotes digestion, reduces blood pressure, strengthens immune system, improves blood circulation, strengthens the muscles. Strengthens gastrointestinal function, expands blood vessels.
Cooking time approx. 30 min
Calories p. portion: 256
2 portions
Allergens: EN

Quantity of ingredients:
Lentils 3/8 lbs - 6oz / 175g. (recommended)
Sesame oil 2 table spoons / 30g. (recommended)
Carrot 1 piece / 100g. (recommended)
Onion (shallot) 1 piece / 15g. (yes)
Water 1 1/2 cups / 200g. (yes)
Ginger fresh 2 slices / 1g. (yes)
Salt 1 pinch / 0,5g. (little)
Soy sauce 1 teaspoon / 3g. (yes)
Parsley 1 teaspoon (chopped) / 3g. (yes)
Thyme 1 teaspoon / 3g. (yes)
Basil 1 table spoon / 5g. (yes)

Cooking instructions:
Soak the lentils overnight.
in a hot pot, carrot, onion and a little ginger fry, pour water. Add the lentils and cook until soft. Add salt or soy sauce and cook for another 10 minutes.
Stir in parsley before serving; Sprinkle thyme or basil over it.
Variant: Other herbs such as sage, rosemary or lovage allow a variety of flavors.

9.31 Japanese algae soup

Reduces blood pressure, strengthens immune system, prevents cancer, reduces radiation damage. Promotes digestion. Detoxifying and stimulates the immune system.
Cooking time approx. 20 min
Calories p. portion: 47
3 portions
Allergens:

Quantity of ingredients:
Wakame 1 oz / 25g. (yes)
Water 2 cup / 450g. (yes)
Onion (shallot) 1-2 pcs. / 30g. (yes)
Radish (white, green, purple-red) 1/8 lbs - 2oz / 50g. (recommended)
Carrot 2 pieces / 180g. (recommended)
Miso 2 table spoons / 20g. (yes)
Parsley 2 table spoons / 20g. (yes)
Onion (spring onion) 1 table spoon (sliced)

Cooking instructions:
Soak wakame in water for a few minutes, remove and bring the water to the boil. Add finely chopped onions and wakame, radishes and carrots, cut into thin strips, and simmer for another 10 minutes. Dissolve miso in a little cooled cooking water and add it at the end. Sprinkle with parsley and spring onions.

9.32 Lasagne with tofu cream

Harmonizes spleen and stomach, reduces Flatulence, protects the digestive system. Good to fight lack of appetite, flatulence, inflammatory bowel disease, stomach ulcers, rheumatism, heartburn, twelffinger intestinal ulcers.
Cooking time approx. 45 min
Calories p. portion: 301
4 portions
Allergens: ACEG

Quantity of ingredients:
Soy Tofu 7/8 lbs / 400g. (yes)
Chicken egg 2 pieces / 100g. (yes)
Onion white 2 pieces / 120g. (yes)
Tomato 1/4 lbs - 4oz / 100g. (recommended)
Oregano dried 1 pinch / 1g. (yes)
Marjoram 1 pinch / 1g. (yes)
Peppers powder 1 pinch / 1g. (yes)
Salt 1 pinch / 1g. (little)
Noodles (wheat, lasagne) with egg 3/8 lbs - 6oz / 150g. (yes)
Edam cheese 1/8 lbs - 2oz / 50g. (yes)

Cooking instructions:
Tofu cream: Mix tofu with eggs, onions, small tomatoes, oregano, marjoram, peppers and some sea salt put into a smooth mass using a

kitchen machine with a knife or a blender.

Lasagne: Place 1/5 of the tofu cream in a casserole dish (25x15cm), cover with 3 lasagna leaves, repeat this process twice, and then finish the last fifth of the tofu cream over the pastry plates. Sprinkle with a little grated Edam and bake in the oven at 175°C/347°F for about 1/2 hour.

9.33 Lentils and rice stew

Promotes spleen and kidney, is very nutritious, reduces blood pressure, strengthens immune system. Good to fight blood circulation disorders, thromboses, risk of embolism, high blood pressure, a headache. Strengthens heart and kidney, diuretic, calms the stomach, promotes digestion.
Cooking time approx. 25 min
Calories p. portion: 232
3 portions
Allergens: LNO

Quantity of ingredients:
Lentils 1/4 lbs - 4oz / 100g. (recommended)
Water 5 cups / 500g. (yes)
Rice variety any 1 cup / 120g. (yes)
Sesame oil 1 table spoon / 10g. (recommended)
Carrot 2 pieces / 150g. (recommended)
Celery sticks 2 rods / 20g. (recommended)
Cumin (Caraway seed) 1 pinch / 0,2g. (yes)
Salt 1 pinch / 0,5g. (little)
Vinegar (Apple vinegar) 1 dash / 2g. (yes)
Parsley 2 table spoons / 18g. (yes)

Cooking instructions:
Soak the dry lentils the day before.
Heat sesame oil in a hot pot; cut carrot and celery into small pieces and sauté; add rice, a pinch of cumin and lentils and heat till it boils.
If the lenses are soft, add salt; season with a little vinegar and garnish with parsley.

Variant: In summer you can omit the cumin and add fresh green peas, Chinese cabbage or celery.

9.34 Melanzani with olive oil and turmeric

improves blood circulation, reduces inflammation, relieves pain, promotes digestion, helps to digest fat, supports urination, reduces blood pressure.
Cooking time approx. 30 min
Calories p. portion: 432
2 portions
Allergens: A

Quantity of ingredients:
Aubergine 2 pieces / 300g. (yes)
Olive oil 4 table spoons / 60g. (yes)
Tomato 4 pieces / 200g. (recommended)
Turmeric (yellow root) 1/2 teaspoon / 1g. (recommended)
Ground 1 pinch / 1g. (yes)
Salt 1 pinch / 1g. (little)
White bread (wheat bread) 4 slices / 80g. (little)

Cooking instructions:
Cut the melanzani into slices and spread them with the tomatoes on a baking tray. Sprinkle with olive oil and then with turmeric, caraway and salt. Bake them in the tube 20 min.
Serve with the white bread.

9.35 Minestrone

Diuretic, Supports urination. Promotes digestion, Helps to digest fat, Supports urination, reduces blood pressure. strengthens immune system.
Cooking time approx. 30 min
Calories p. portion: 211
4 portions
Allergens: GL

Quantity of ingredients:
Onion (shallot) 2 pieces / 40g. (yes)
Sunflower oil 1 teaspoon / 10g. (yes)
Water 2 cup / 480g. (yes)
Carrot 2 pieces / 120g. (recommended)
Savoy cabbage / kale Handful / 15g. (recommended)
Beans (green, fresh) Handful / 20g. (recommended)
Celery sticks 3 pieces / 20g. (recommended)
Peas, green 4 table spoons / 30g. (yes)

Zucchini 1 piece / 200g. (recommended)
Rice variety any 1 cup / 120g. (yes)
Bay leaf 3 leaves / 1g. (yes)
Sunflower oil 1 table spoon / 10g. (yes)
Salt 1 pinch / 1g. (little)
Tomato 3 pieces / 150g. (recommended)
Thyme 1 Twig / 3g. (yes)
Parmesan 2 table spoons / 18g. (yes)
Basil 4 leaves / 2g. (yes)

Cooking instructions:
Fry the onion in oil in a glassy saucepan and add water. Add vegetables, rice and salt and simmer gently. If the vegetables are firm, add tomatoes, a small sprig of thyme, basil and bay leaf and leave to simmer. Serve with Parmesan.

9.36 Oat flakes with aromatic spices

Stops diarrhea, promotes digestion, appetizing, harmonizes the stomach, relieves diarrhea, strengthens immune system, detoxifying and stimulating the immune system.
Cooking time approx. 25 min
Calories p. portion: 280
3 portions
Allergens: AH

Quantity of ingredients:
Oat flakes (whole grain) 1 cup / 125g. (recommended)
Walnuts 1 table spoon / 15g. (yes)
Hazelnuts 1 table spoon / 15g. (yes)
Water 1 1/2 cups / 240g. (yes)
Wakame 1 inch / 2g. (yes)
Apple (sweet) 1 piece / 220g. (recommended)
Cardamom 3-4 capsules / 2g. (yes)
Lemon Balm (fresh) 3-4 leaves / 3g. (recommended)
Acerola fruit nectar or powder 1 teaspoon / 2g. (little)

Cooking instructions:
Roast oatmeal and nuts. Add hot water. Add cardamom, wakame and cook for 20 min. Add grated apple, acerola and lemon herb.

9.37 Oatmeal soup with spring onion and carrots

Reduces blood pressure, strengthens immune system, prevents cancer, reduces radiation damage, stimulates digestion, reduces pain, stimulates appetite, dissolves stagnation.
Cooking time approx. 30 min
Calories p. portion: 135
3 portions
Allergens: AG

Quantity of ingredients:
Oat 6 table spoons / 48g. (yes)
Carrot 2 pieces / 200g. (recommended)
Butter organic 1 table spoon / 15g. (yes)
Nutmeg 1 pinch / 1g. (yes)
Lovage 1 stem / 15g. (yes)
Onion (spring onion) 2 pieces / 40g. (yes)
Water 2 cup / 480g. (yes)

Cooking instructions:
Roast the oats in butter, add salt and spices, pour in water and heat till it boils. After 10 min. add the grated carrots and lovage, cook for 10 minutes. Finely add chopped onion.

9.38 Paprika turkey with rice and lettuce

Strengthens blood and bone marrow.
Cooking time approx. 1 hour
Calories p. portion: 391
6 portions
Allergens: AG

Quantity of ingredients:
Olive oil 2 table spoons / 20g. (yes)
Onion white 1 piece / 60g. (yes)
Peppers (rose peppers) 2 table spoons / 14g. (yes)
Chicken meat 1 piece / 800g. (yes)
Water 1 cup / 250g. (yes)
Salt 1 pinch / 1g. (little)
Spelled wholemeal flour 1 table spoon / 7g. (yes)
Sour cream 15% fat 5/8 lbs - 8oz / 250g. (recommended)
Water 6 cups / 400g. (yes)
Rice Basmati 1 cup / 120g. (yes)
Salt 1 pinch / 1g. (little)

Lettuce 1 piece / 200g. (recommended)
Olive oil 2 table spoons / 20g. (yes)
Lemon juice 1/2 piece / 15g. (little)
Herbs various 2 table spoons / 6g. (yes)

Cooking instructions:
Heat the oil in a saucepan and fry the onions in a golden yellow.
Sprinkle plenty of peppers over the onion and stir well so that it does
not burn. Put the pot aside.
In a casserole, fry the chicken parts from one side; turn the meat over,
spread the onion above and fry the chicken parts from the other side.
As soon as they have taken on a deep red color, pour the vegetable
broth and heat till it boils.
Season with salt, reduce the heat and stew the chicken for 45 minutes
or until cooked.
Put the poultry parts together with cooking liquid in a bowl and set
aside.
Add 2 to 3 tbsp of flour to the casserole and gradually add the cooking
solution again, stirring constantly until the sauce is thickened.
Stir in the sour cream or yoghurt, put the poultry pieces back into the
pot and heat again well, but do not boil.
Place the rice with the salted water, bring to the boil and simmer until
the rice is tender.
Wash and dry the lettuce. Pluck small and put in a bowl.
In a cup, mix the olive oil, the lemon juice, the salt and fresh chopped
herbs and pour over the salad.

9.39 Polenta with ratatouille

Forcing spleen and stomach, lets urine and bile juice flow. Diuretic,
supports urination. Promotes digestion, helps to digest fat, supports
urination, reduces blood pressure.
Cooking time approx. 30 min
Calories p. portion: 226
4 portions
Allergens: G

Quantity of ingredients:
Corn Grease (Polenta) 1 cup / 120g. (yes)
Water 1 1/2 cups / 240g. (yes)
Aubergine 1 piece (large) / 200g. (yes)
Zucchini 2 pieces / 500g. (recommended)
Onion white 2 pieces / 120g. (yes)

Tomato 2 pieces (blended) / 200g. (recommended)
Olive oil 2 table spoons / 20g. (yes)
Salt 1 pinch / 0,5g. (little)
Parsley 1 table spoon (chopped) / 8g. (yes)
Thyme 1/2 teaspoon / 1g. (yes)
Onion (spring onion) 2 table spoons (chopped) / 12g. (yes)
Basil 4 leaves / 2g. (yes)
Parmesan 2 table spoons / 20g. (yes)

Cooking instructions:
Use double the amount of water to polenta, add salt and oil and heat till
it boils. Stir in polenta, stirring constantly. Take off the fire and let it
swell for 20 minutes. Meanwhile, cut the onion, fry in a saucepan with
hot oil. Add the diced zucchini, tomatoes and melanzani and simmer for
about 20 minutes. Add basil, thyme, salt.
Coat baking tray with oil, apply polenta evenly and wait until it gets
stronger.
Add the cooked ratatouille to polenta, portion and then put in the oven
for a few minutes (possibly with grated parmesan).
Sprinkle with fresh parsley and finely chopped spring onion.
The valuable tip: The Polenta sections are ideal for on the go.

9.40 Porridge with raisins and sake

Strengthens immune system, improves blood circulation, improves
medication effect, stimulates appetite, detoxifies the skin, stimulates
nerves, frees breathing, increases body temperature, promotes
perspiration.
Cooking time approx. 10 min
Calories p. portion: 427
1 portions
Allergens: AGO

Quantity of ingredients:
Oat flakes (whole grain) 8 table spoons / 60g. (recommended)
Water 1/2 cup / 125g. (yes)
Cow's milk (whole milk 3.5% fat) 1/2 cup / 125g. (yes)
Salt 1 pinch / 1g. (little)
Cream, sweet 30% 2 table spoons / 20g. (little)
Raisins 1 table spoon / 15g. (yes)
Sake 1 table spoon / 10g. (little)

Cooking instructions:
Heat water and milk and a pinch of salt till it boils. Sprinkle in 4 tablespoons of coarse rolled oats and cook to a pulp, add 4 tablespoons of fine oatmeal, allow to simmer. Arrange in a preheated bowl and top with cream.
Add raisins and sake.

9.41 Potato pancakes

Promotes spleen, reduces inflammation, improves digestion, regenerates skin, supports urination, calms nerves and stomach, laxative, antiparasitic.
Cooking time approx. 15 min
Calories p. portion: 893
1 portions
Allergens: ACG

Quantity of ingredients:
Potato (mealy) 5/8 lbs - 8oz / 250g. (yes)
Wheat flour 1/2 oz / 10g. (yes)
Chicken egg 1 piece / 35g. (yes)
Rapeseed oil 2 table spoons / 20g. (recommended)
Salt 1 pinch / 1g. (little)
Cream sour 20% 1/8 lbs - 2oz / 50g. (recommended)
Salt 1 pinch / 1g. (little)
Herbs various 1 table spoon / 10g. (yes)

Cooking instructions:
Grater the peeled potatoes finely, add the remaining ingredients, mix well and salt. Heat the oil and add small flat cakes to the pan with the spoon. Roast the potato pancakes on both sides crispy golden brown. Place them on the plate with sour cream, salt and sprinkle with herbs.

9.42 Pumpkin soup

Promotes digestion, forcing spleen and stomach, reduces blood pressure, strengthens immune system, prevents cancer, reduces radiation damage, improves digestion, regenerates skin, lowers cholesterol, reduces blood glucose, protects liver.
Cooking time approx. 1 hour
Calories p. portion: 105
3 portions
Allergens:

Quantity of ingredients:
Pumpkin 3/4 lbs / 300g. (yes)
Carrot 2 pieces / 100g. (recommended)
Potato 2 pieces / 120g. (yes)
Olive oil 1 table spoon / 10g. (yes)
Onion white 1 piece / 50g. (yes)
Water 1 cup / 120g. (yes)
Parsley 1 table spoon / 7g. (yes)
Anise (Common Fennel) 1 pinch / 1g. (yes)
Salt 1 pinch / 1g. (little)

Cooking instructions:
Add the olive oil to the pan, add the diced pumpkin, diced carrots and potatoes. Roast them shortly, add the finely chopped onion, fill with water, add enough water to cover the vegetables at least 3 finger-widths. Boil at low heat.

Season with sea salt, add small cutted parsley, a pinch of anise (little). Allow to simmer for about 35 minutes. Then purée the soup and add some water, depending on the consistency of the soup.

9.43 Quick zucchini soup

Diuretic, supports urination. Strengthens gastrointestinal function, expands blood vessels, prevents cancer, prevents diseases (in the elderly). Stimulates liver function, detoxifying.
Cooking time approx. 10 min
Calories p. portion: 42
4 portions
Allergens:

Quantity of ingredients:
Zucchini 2-3 pieces / 500g. (recommended)
Onion white 1 piece / 50g. (yes)
Corn germ oil 2 table spoons / 6g. (recommended)
Parsley 1 table spoon / 7g. (yes)
Chives 1 teaspoon / 3g. (yes)
Water 2 cup / 400g. (yes)

Cooking instructions:
Fry chopped onion in oil. Add sliced zucchini and sauté well. Pour with water. Chop parsley and chives, add and puree everything.

9.44 Radish with horseradish

Stimulates liver function, detoxifying. Promotes digestion, improves blood circulation, supports urination, reduces thirst.
Cooking time approx. 30 min
Calories p. portion: 196
2 portions
Allergens: GNO

Quantity of ingredients:
Butter organic 1 table spoon / 8g. (yes)
Radish (white, green, purple-red) 1/2 piece / 50g. (recommended)
Water 2 table spoons / 10g. (yes)
Lemon juice 2 table spoons / 20g. (little)
White wine 2 table spoons / 20g. (little)
Pepper powder (hot) 1 pinch / 0,2g. (yes)
Sesame oil 1 teaspoon / 3g. (recommended)
Radish horseradish 2 table spoons / 20g. (recommended)
Salt 1 pinch / 0,5g. (little)
Parsley 1 Bunch (chopped) / 80g. (yes)
Rice long grain rice 1/2 cup / 60g. (yes)
Water 3 cups / 300g. (yes)
Salt 1 pinch / 0,5g. (little)

Cooking instructions:
In a hot pan melt the butter, sautéed into stripes cut radish. Add cold water, lemon juice, white wine, a pinch of rose paprika and stir in the sesame oil; with 2 - 3 tablespoons fresh grated horseradish (alternatively 1 teaspoon from the glass), salt to taste; Sprinkle with chopped parsley.

Place the rice with the water, salt and cook for about 15 minutes.

9.45 Radish with spring onions and carrots

Reduces blood pressure, strengthens immune system, prevents cancer, reduces radiation damage, forcing spleen and stomach, lets urine and bile juice flow, strengthens brain cells. Strengthens gastrointestinal function, expands blood vessels.
Cooking time approx. 30 min
Calories p. portion: 246
2 portions
Allergens: EG

Quantity of ingredients:
Carrot 2 pieces / 200g. (recommended)
Radish black 1/2 piece / 100g. (recommended)
Ginger powder 1 knife tip / 0,2g. (yes)
Onion (spring onion) 1 piece / 20g. (yes)
Salt 1 pinch / 0,5g. (little)
Soy sauce 1 dash / 2g. (yes)
Lemon juice 2 table spoons / 16g. (little)
Curcuma 1 pinch / 0,2g. (yes)
Pepper powder (hot) 1 pinch / 0,2g. (yes)
Butter organic 1 teaspoon / 3g. (yes)
Water 1 cup / 250g. (yes)
Corn Grease (Polenta) 1 cup / 100g. (yes)
Salt 1 pinch / 0,5g. (little)

Cooking instructions:
Cook finely chopped carrots, black or white finely chopped radish, a pinch of grated ginger. Steam for 10 minutes, then strain.
In the meantime stir in chopped spring onions, salt, soy sauce, a little lemon juice, a pinch of turmeric or rose paprika and a piece of butter.
Garnish:
Stir the polenta into a pot of hot water, stirring constantly, until the polenta has the desired texture. Pull the polenta off the fire and let it swell for about 10 minutes.

9.46 Radish, apple and yogurt fresh food

Stops diarrhea, promotes digestion, appetizing, detoxifying, supports urination, reduces thirst, prevents cancer, strengthens body cells, dissolves stagnation.
Cooking time approx. 10 min
Calories p. portion: 77
2 portions
Allergens: G

Quantity of ingredients:
Yogurt (natural, 3.5% fat) 5 table spoons / 50g. (yes)
Lemon juice 1/2 teaspoon / 2g. (little)
Salt 1 pinch / 0,5g. (little)
Pepper white (ground) 1 pinch / 0,1g. (yes)
Radish (white, green, purple-red) 1/4 lbs - 4oz / 100g. (recommended)
Apple (sweet) 1 piece / 150g. (recommended)
Parsley 2 table spoons / 18g. (yes)

Cooking instructions:
Mix yoghurt with lemon juice, salt and white pepper.
Wash radish and apple, peel and finely grate. Mix with the yoghurt sauce, let it pass briefly. Sprinkle with chopped parsley.

9.47 Radish juice

Promotes digestion, detoxifying (for example alcohol poisoning), improves blood circulation, supports urination, reduces thirst, prevents cancer, strengthens body cells.
Cooking time approx. 10 min
Calories p. portion: 9
1 portions
Allergens:

Quantity of ingredients:
Radish (white, green, purple-red) 1/2 piece / 50g. (recommended)
Water 1 cup / 120g. (yes)

Cooking instructions:
Make the radish juice with the juicer or buy it at the food store.
The fresh press juice is extracted from the root.
For healing purposes one prefers the black radish because of its sharpness.
The pungent taste is due to the mustard oils in the radish juice.
They stimulate bile-juice production in the liver. This has two different effects in our body. The appetite and digestion are promoted and alleviates bile and liver disease.
Drink in small sips.

9.48 Rice congee with crushed walnuts

Good to fight blood circulation disorders, high blood pressure, a headache, for the drainage of the body overweight and high blood pressure. Dissolves stones. Warms stomach and spleen, improves blood circulation. Antipyretic.
Cooking time approx. 2 hours and more
Calories p. portion: 406
2 portions
Allergens: H

Quantity of ingredients:
Basic recipe for a rice soup (Congee) 4 cups / 500g. (yes)
Sugar cane sugar 2 table spoons / 20g. (little)
Walnuts 1 cup / 70g. (yes)
Cinnamon ground 1 pinch / 0,2g. (yes)

Cooking instructions:
Cook the basic recipe for rice soup (congee)
Note: The crushed walnuts can be cooked from the beginning.
Variation: Refine with sweet or spicy ingredients as you like. In particular, cinnamon, cloves, and ginger increase the warming effect and wholesomeness.

9.49 Rice congee with honey pear and black sesame

Promotes digestion, supports urination, good to fight blood circulation disorders, thromboses, risk of embolism, high blood pressure, a headache, heart attack and stroke.
Cooking time approx. 10 min - 3 hours
Calories p. portion: 158
2 portions
Allergens: N

Quantity of ingredients:
Basic recipe for a rice soup (Congee) 1 1/2 cups / 240g. (yes)
Pear 2 pieces / 300g. (recommended)
Sesame, black 1 teaspoon / 3g. (yes)

Cooking instructions:
Cook rice congee according to basic recipe.
Fill pot with 3 cm of water and heat till it boils. Quarter the pears (with the skin and seeds) and simmer them covered with black sesame for 10 minutes. Mix with the rice.

9.50 Rice noodle soup with shiitake mushrooms

Very light and powerful. Strengthens the immune system.
Cooking time approx. 20 min
Calories p. portion: 66
2 portions
Allergens: L

Quantity of ingredients:
Rice noodles 2 handful / 20g. (yes)
Shiitake, dried 4-6 pieces / 5g. (yes)
Basic recipe for a vegetable soup (nutritious) 1 1/2 cups / 240g. (yes)
Chinese cabbage 1 cup / 60g. (recommended)
Lovage 1 teaspoon / 3g. (yes)
Miso 2 table spoons / 18g. (yes)

Cooking instructions:
Soak rice noodles and shiitake mushrooms separately in cold water.
Heat the vegetable broth and add the soaked shiitake mushrooms cut
into strips and simmer gently. Cut Chinese cabbage into noodles, add
lovage green and rice noodles and let it steep for a while. Before
serving, stir in Miso dissolved in a little cooled water. Recommendation:
Suitable at the beginning of each meal, also for breakfast

9.51 Rice soup with grated carrots and fresh herbs

Diuretic, warming the body from the inside, expands blood vessels,
strengthens the muscles, regulates internal organs functions, reduces
blood pressure, strengthens immune system, prevents cancer, reduces
radiation damage. Promotes digestion.
Cooking time approx. 5 min
Calories p. portion: 131
4 portions
Allergens: EG

Quantity of ingredients:
Rice wild (nature rice) 1 cup / 100g. (recommended)
Water 6 cups / 700g. (yes)
Carrot 1 piece / 100g. (recommended)
Soy sauce 1 dash / 2g. (yes)
Butter organic 1 teaspoon / 3g. (yes)
Ground 1 pinch / 0,3g. (yes)
Curcuma 1 pinch / 0,2g. (yes)
Herbs various 1 teaspoon (chopped) / 3g. (yes)

Cooking instructions:
In a portion of rice congee according to basic recipe, softly cook a
grated carrot, add butter and soy sauce.
Sprinkle with fresh herbs.
Spices and herbs: black cumin, turmeric, cardamom, parsley, sage,
thyme, basil, rosemary.

Winter: parsnip, celery, onion, leek, pumpkin
Summer: tomatoes, zucchini, spring onion, radishes, arugula.

9.52 Rice with stewed vegetables

Reduces blood pressure, strengthens immune system, prevents cancer, reduces radiation damage, extremely low fat content, good to fight blood circulation disorders, thrombose, risk of embolism, a headache, heart attack and stroke. Is diuretic.
Cooking time approx. 20 min
Calories p. portion: 166
2 portions
Allergens: L

Quantity of ingredients:
Rice variety any 1/2 cup / 60g. (yes)
Water 3 cups / 300g. (yes)
Lemon peel 1 piece / 3g. (yes)
Water 1/2 cup / 0g. (yes)
Carrot 2 pieces / 180g. (recommended)
Celery sticks 1/2 piece / 5g. (recommended)
Champignon 1/2 cup / 50g. (yes)
Cress 2 table spoons / 20g. (yes)
Linseed oil 1 dash / 3g. (recommended)

Cooking instructions:
Cook rice according to basic recipe with a piece of lemon peel.
Steam chopped carrots, celery and mushrooms until soft.
Then sprinkle with cress. Then add a dash of high quality cold oil.

9.53 Roasted millet with Celery sticks

Promotes spleen and kidney, diuretic, promoting metabolism.
Cooking time approx. 30 min
Calories p. portion: 400
2 portions
Allergens: L

Quantity of ingredients:
Millet 1 cup / 120g. (yes)
Water 1 1/2 cups / 240g. (yes)
Celery sticks 2 rods / 50g. (recommended)
Herbs various 1 table spoon / 10g. (yes)
Water 2 table spoons / 30g. (yes)

Salt 1 pinch / 1g. (little)
Sage 3-4 leaves / 2g. (yes)
Cress 1 teaspoon / 3g. (yes)

Cooking instructions:
Roast millet briefly, pour over water, heat till it boils and let stand for 20 min. to swell.

Cut celery into small pieces and mix with water, salt and fresh herbs and cook for 10 min. Add to the millet. Sprinkle fresh sage or watercress over it.

9.54 Roasted millet with plum compote

Supports urination, promotes spleen and kidney, strengthens the defense. Good to fight fungi infections.
Cooking time approx. 30 min
Calories p. portion: 139
4 portions
Allergens:

Quantity of ingredients:
Millet 1 cup / 120g. (yes)
Water 1 1/2 cups / 250g. (yes)
Plum 1 1/2 cups / 250g. (recommended)
Vanilla pod 1 pinch / 1g. (yes)
Water 5/8 lbs - 8oz / 250g. (yes)
Cinnamon ground 1 pinch / 1g. (yes)
Acerola fruit nectar or powder 1/2 teaspoon / 1g. (little)

Cooking instructions:
Roast millet briefly, pour over water, heat till it boils and let stand for 20 min. to swell.

Cook plums with water, vanilla and cinnamon 10 min. then strain. Add acerola and add to the millet.

9.55 Russian kasha with white cabbage

Promotes digestion, relieves pain, detoxifying, promotes digestion, stimulates appetite, dissolves stagnation, stimulates blood production and metabolism, reduces fat.
Cooking time approx. 30 min
Calories p. portion: 250
2 portions
Allergens: AG

Quantity of ingredients:
Buckwheat whole grain 1 cup / 130g. (yes)
Water 1 1/2 cups / 240g. (yes)
Nutmeg 1 pinch / 1g. (yes)
Salt 1 pinch / 1g. (little)
Parsley 1 table spoon / 10g. (yes)
Ground 1 pinch / 2g. (yes)
Butter organic 1 teaspoon / 3g. (yes)
White cabbage Handful / 20g. (recommended)

Cooking instructions:
Roast buckwheat golden yellow; add boiling water, heat till it boils briefly and then let it swell until soft; Grate the white cabbage finely and fold in. Season with nutmeg, a little salt; some parsley, cumin and butter at the end.

9.56 Salmon on tomato-spinach

Promotes bowel movement, improves blood circulation, forcing spleen and bowel, strengthens blood, reduces inflammation, improves digestion, regenerates skin, supports urination, lowers cholesterol, promotes sweating, dissolves stagnation.
Cooking time approx. 1 hour
Calories p. portion: 365
6 portions
Allergens: D

Quantity of ingredients:
Potato 1,1 lbs / 500g. (yes)
Salt 1 pinch / 1g. (little)
Salmon 1,3 lbs / 600g. (recommended)
Rapeseed oil 2 teaspoons / 24g. (recommended)
Tomato 1/4 lbs - 4oz / 100g. (recommended)
Spinach 1,5 lbs / 700g. (yes)

Salt 1 pinch / 1g. (little)
Pine nuts 4 table spoons / 40g. (yes)
Leek 1/4 lbs - 4oz / 120g. (yes)
Olive oil 4 table spoons / 40g. (yes)
Salt 1 pinch / 1g. (little)
Pepper white (ground) 1 pinch / 0,5g. (yes)

Cooking instructions:
Peel the potato and cut into cubes, cook in salted water.
Cut the salmon into portions and fry slowly and evenly in a frying pan
from both sides, seasoned with salt and pepper, then add the pine nuts
and lightly roast.
Blanch spinach in salted water.
Lightly sweat the finely chopped leek with a little rapeseed oil, add the
blanched spinach and heat evenly.
Just before serving, add the halved cocktail tomatoes to the spinach
and season the vegetables well with salt and pepper.
Arrange the spinach and leek tomato bed with the potatoes, add the
salmon and sprinkle with the salted pine nuts.
Drizzle with a little olive oil and serve the dish.

9.57 Semolina soup with vegetables

Reduces blood pressure, strengthens immune system, prevents cancer,
forcing spleen, dissolves stagnation, promotes weight loss. Good to
fight immunodeficiency, loss of appetite, flatulence, high blood
pressure, depressions, diabetes, diarrhea, rheumatism, heartburn,
twelffinger intestinal ulcers.
Cooking time approx. 20 min
Calories p. portion: 105
3 portions
Allergens: AGL

Quantity of ingredients:
Basic recipe for a vegetable soup (nutritious) 2 cup / 500g. (yes)
Wheat semolina 2 table spoons / 20g. (yes)
Lovage 1/2 teaspoon / 2g. (yes)
Basil (fresh) 1/2 teaspoon / 1g. (yes)
Nutmeg 1 pinch / 0,1g. (yes)
Carrot 1/4 lbs - 4oz / 100g. (recommended)
Celery root 1/8 lbs - 2oz / 50g. (recommended)
Cream, sweet 30% 2 table spoons / 30g. (little)
Parsley 1 table spoon / 10g. (yes)

Cooking instructions:
Roast wheat grits without fat in a pan. Roast the chopped carrots and celery briefly. Add the vegetable soup (Basic recipe for a vegetable soup). Season with lovage, nutmeg and let it 10 min. simmer.
Stir in the cream before serving and garnish with parsley.

9.58 Sliced chicken with walnuts and sherry

Strengthens blood, strengthens bone marrow, strengthens gastrointestinal function, expands blood vessels, prevents cancer, promotes perspiration, reduces blood lipids, stimulates.
Cooking time approx. 25 min
Calories p. portion: 304
4 portions
Allergens: EGHN

Quantity of ingredients:
Butter organic 2 table spoons / 35g. (yes)
Walnuts 2 table spoons / 25g. (yes)
Ginger fresh 1/2 teaspoon / 2g. (yes)
Onion (shallot) 2 pieces / 40g. (yes)
Salt 1 pinch / 1g. (little)
Chicken meat 3/4 lbs / 300g. (yes)
Peppers powder 1 pinch / 1g. (yes)
Sesame, white 1 teaspoon / 2g. (yes)
Black fungus mushroom 4 pieces / 3g. (yes)
Shiitake, dried 4 pieces / 5g. (yes)
Soy sauce 1 dash / 3g. (yes)
Rice (whole grain) 1 cup / 120g. (recommended)
Water 6 cups / 550g. (yes)
Salt 1 pinch / 1g. (little)

Cooking instructions:
Heat butter or sesame oil in a hot pan; Sauté walnuts, copious grated ginger, chopped shallots or onions; Add the salt and the sliced chicken and sauté everything; Rose paprika, roasted sesame, soaked black fungus, shiitake mushrooms or mushrooms; with a shot sherry; infuse with water; Simmer for 5 to 10 minutes until the meat is cooked; Season with soy sauce.
Place the rice in salted water, heat till it boils and let it simmer over low heat for about 15 minutes.
This fits: lamb's lettuce, Radicchio

9.59 Soup with cucumbers and tomatoes

Diuretic, detoxifying, suppresses conversion of sugar into fat, lowers cholesterol. Promotes digestion, helps to digest fat, supports urination, reduces blood pressure, calms nerves and stomach.
Cooking time approx. 10 min
Calories p. portion: 137
2 portions
Allergens: CO

Quantity of ingredients:
Cucumber 1 piece / 300g. (recommended)
Tomato 4 pieces (very ripe) / 200g. (recommended)
Onion white 1 piece / 50g. (yes)
Peppers 1/2 piece (green) / 10g. (recommended)
Salt 1 pinch / 0,5g. (little)
Vinegar (Apple vinegar) 1 dash / 2g. (yes)
Water 1 cup / 120g. (yes)
Chicken egg 2 pieces / 120g. (yes)

Cooking instructions:
Puree all ingredients in the blender. Cool in the fridge. When serving, sprinkle with chopped breadcrumbs and finely chopped boiled egg.

9.60 Spelled with fruit and nuts

Stops diarrhea, promotes digestion, appetizing, relieves fatigue, anti-inflammatory (gastrointestinal). Good to fight tumor lesions and leukemia, is antiallergic in food allergies, regulates metabolism, lowers blood glucose and cholesterol.
Cooking time approx. 1 1/2 hours
Calories p. portion: 290
3 portions
Allergens: AH

Quantity of ingredients:
Spelled grain 1 cup / 120g. (yes)
Water 1 cup / 50g. (yes)
Apple (sweet) 1 piece / 220g. (recommended)
Apricot 1 piece / 200g. (little)
Peaches 1 piece / 120g. (recommended)
Cinnamon ground 1 pinch / 1g. (yes)
Cardamom 1 pinch / 1g. (yes)
Salt 1 pinch / 1g. (little)

Strawberries 1 cup / 120g. (recommended)
Almond puree 1 table spoon / 15g. (yes)
Cocoa 1 pinch / 1g. (yes)
Walnuts 1 table spoon / 10g. (yes)

Cooking instructions:
Put spelled in hot water and cook.

Then: Give sweet chopped fruit (apples, apricots, peaches) in a little hot water, with a little cinnamon, sauté briefly; ground cardamom and / or coriander, a small pinch of salt, the boiled spelled, berries after season. Put some cocoa and roasted nuts over it.

9.61 Strawberry yoghurt and almond puree mix

Relieves pain and inflammation in rheumatism. Good to fight acute or chronic constipation of the intestine. Little laxative. Relieves pain, detoxifying, bactericide.
Cooking time approx. 5 min
Calories p. portion: 134
3 portions
Allergens: GH

Quantity of ingredients:
Yogurt (natural, 1.5% fat) 5/8 oz / 200g. (yes)
Strawberries 1,5 lbs / 700g. (recommended)
Honey 1 teaspoon / 3g. (little)
Acerola fruit nectar or powder 1 teaspoon / 2g. (little)
Almond puree 2 teaspoons / 6g. (yes)

Cooking instructions:
Puree yoghurt, strawberries, acerola, honey and almond paste in a blender.

9.62 Sweet polenta with peach

Supports erythrocyte production, relieves fatigue, relaxes. Forcing spleen and stomach, lets urine and bile juice flow, prevents the aging process, strengthens brain cells. Strengths spleen and stomach. Promotes digestion.
Cooking time approx. 20 min
Calories p. portion: 330
2 portions
Allergens: GHO

Quantity of ingredients:
Water 1 1/2 cups / 240g. (yes)
Corn Grease (Polenta) 1 cup / 100g. (yes)
Butter organic 1/2 teaspoon / 2g. (yes)
Barley malt 1/2 teaspoon / 2g. (yes)
Cinnamon ground 1 pinch / 0,2g. (yes)
Cardamom 1 pinch / 0,2g. (yes)
Salt 1 pinch / 0,5g. (little)
Lemon 1 dash / 1g. (little)
Raisins 2 table spoons / 20g. (yes)
Apple juice (natural cloudy) until covered / 10g. (yes)
Peaches 2 pieces / 240g. (recommended)
Hazelnuts 2 table spoons / 20g. (yes)

Cooking instructions:
Heat water till it boils. Stir in the polenta with a whisk and until tender;
add some butter or cream, barley malt or maple syrup, cinnamon, some
cardamom, a pinch of salt, a few drops of lemon juice and stir well.

Separately prepare a compote:
In a hot pot, simmer raisins in some apple or apricot juice for a few
minutes; add fully ripe peaches chopped and heat; pour over the
polenta served on plates; sprinkle with roasted nuts as desired.

9.63 Sweet potato pancakes with basil pesto

Strengthens the immune system, reduces fat, Improves digestion,
calms nerves and stomach, dissolves stones, improves blood
circulation, strengthens the muscles, antioxidativ.
Cooking time approx. 30 min
Calories p. portion: 625
3 portions
Allergens: ACH

Quantity of ingredients:
Sweet potato 4 pieces / 500g. (yes)
Onion read 1/2 piece / 30g. (yes)
Basil 1 table spoon / 10g. (yes)
Chicken egg 2 pieces / 140g. (yes)
Spelled wholemeal flour 3 oz / 80g. (yes)

Salt 1 pinch / 0,5g. (little)
Olive oil 1/4 cup / 20g. (yes)
Salt 1 teaspoon (coarse) / 3g. (little)
Basil Handful / 15g. (yes)
Parsley Handful / 15g. (yes)
Garlic 2 cloves / 3g. (yes)
Walnuts 1/8 lbs - 2oz / 60g. (yes)
Olive oil 2 table spoons / 20g. (yes)

Cooking instructions:
Sweet Potato Buffer: Wash the sweet potato thoroughly, but do not peel, and grate into a large bowl. Add onion, basil, egg and flour, mix well and sprinkle with salt. The mixture can be formed into buffers. Bake in a preheated tube on a baking tray coated with oil for 4 to 5 minutes on both sides.

Basil Pesto: Add the salt, chopped basil and parsley and crushed garlic in a small bowl and crush (if available, use the mortar). Add the grated walnuts. While stirring, add enough olive oil until the desired consistency is achieved.

9.64 Tea from bearberry leaf

Good to fight urinary tract infections. Inhibits growth of bacteria, viruses and fungi, easily dehydrating.
Cooking time approx. 10 min
Calories p. portion: 0
4 portions
Allergens:

Quantity of ingredients:
Bearberry leaf 2 table spoons / 8g. (recommended)
Water 2 cup / 500g. (yes)

Cooking instructions:
Heat the water till it boils and put it aside. Add grape leaves and leave for 10 min. to let go. Sweet to taste with honey. Strain when pouring.

9.65 Tea from juniper berry

Promotes digestion, diuretic, dries out, good to fight loss of appetite, diarrhea, dehydrates, gastrointestinal complaints, muscle rheumatism and pyelonephritis, heartburn, germicidal, improves blood circulation.
Cooking time approx. 10 min
Calories p. portion: 10
1 portions
Allergens:

Quantity of ingredients:
Juniper berry 1 teaspoon / 3g. (recommended)
Water 1 cup / 125g. (yes)

Cooking instructions:
A teaspoon of dried juniper berries for a cup of tea. Start cold and bring to the boil. Let it sit for 15 minutes, then strain.
This tea is unsweetened and swallowed, slowly drunk. The amount is enough for one day.

9.66 Tea Green tea

Green tea promotes digestion, supports urination, dissolves mucus, detoxifying, stimulates nerves, reduces inflammation.
Cooking time approx. 10 min
Calories p. portion: 2
1 portions
Allergens:

Quantity of ingredients:
Green tea 1 teaspoon / 2g. (recommended)
Water 1 cup / 120g. (yes)

Cooking instructions:
For each cup you use a teaspoonful or a teabag.
Pour green tea only with 60 to 80 ° C / 140 to 176 °F hot water, otherwise it will be bitter.
If the tea has a stimulating effect, let it draw for two to three minutes. It has a calming effect for a duration of five minutes (no longer, otherwise it will be bitter!).
Another method: Pour the tea leaves with about 70 ° C / 158 °F hot water and pour the water immediately again. Then just pour hot water again. The bitter substances disappear and the tea gets a milder aroma.

9.67 Tea mixture - reducing uric acid

Good to fight gout or rheumatism, joint pain, urinary tract infections, renal colic.
Cooking time approx. 10 min
Calories p. portion: 0
2 portions
Allergens:

Quantity of ingredients:
Tea mixture uric acid lowering 2 teaspoons / 3g. (recommended)
Water 1 cup / 250g. (yes)

Cooking instructions:
Get tea mixture from the pharmacy or health food store.

Brew 2 teaspoons of the mixture with 1/4 liter of boiling water, 10min. let go, strain.

Increased uric acid levels can cause joint pain at the beginning. These are a reaction to the flushing of uric acid out of the body. There should also be a lot of movement in this time in order to speed up and support the elimination process.

9.68 Tea mixture appetizing

Ginger powder is warming, promotes sweating, dissolves stagnation.
Cooking time approx. 10 min
Calories p. portion: 0
4 portions
Allergens:

Quantity of ingredients:
Bitter orange peel 1 teaspoons / 3g. (yes)
Yarrow tea 1 teaspoons / 3g. (yes)
Ginger powder 1g. Or 0,034oz / 1g. (yes)
Horehound leaves 1 teaspoons / 3g. (yes)
Water 2 cups / 500g. (yes)

Cooking instructions:
Brew one tablespoon of tea mixture with half a liter of water and leave for 10 min. to let go. Then strain and drink in small sips before eating.

9.69 Vegetable bowl with tofu and curry on rice

Diuretic, reduces blood glucose. Reduces flatulence, supports digestion. Contains ideal herbal mucus, which provides regeneration of the small and large intestinal flora. Strengthens immune system.
Cooking time approx. 30 min
Calories p. portion: 162
6 portions
Allergens: E

Quantity of ingredients:
Olive oil 2 table spoons / 20g. (yes)
Garlic 2 cloves / 3g. (yes)
Onion white 1 piece / 60g. (yes)
Curry 2 table spoons / 16g. (little)
Water 2 cup / 500g. (yes)
Turnips 2 pieces / 50g. (recommended)
Pumpkin 1 piece / 400g. (yes)
Carrot 1 piece / 100g. (recommended)
Parsnip 1 piece / 150g. (yes)
Potato 1 piece / 70g. (yes)
Sweet potato 1 piece / 70g. (yes)
Cauliflower 1/4 piece / 250g. (recommended)
Broccoli 1/2 piece / 250g. (recommended)
Okra 12 pieces / 200g. (yes)
Soy Tofu 1 piece / 250g. (yes)
Basil 2 table spoons / 12g. (yes)
Salt 1 pinch / 0,5g. (little)

Cooking instructions:
Heat the oil at medium temperature in a large, heavy casserole, add the garlic and onion and sauté with constant stirring. Sprinkle curry powder over it, fry gently for about 5 minutes and make sure that the garlic and curry do not burn. Add the water and heat till it boils. Gradually peel all vegetables, dice and add, starting with the varieties that need the longest cooking time. Once the water has boiled again, reduce the heat and simmer the vegetables for about 15 minutes. When it is almost soft. Add the cauliflower and broccoli florets and the okra and cook the stew for another 10 to 15 minutes. Add the tofu during the last 5 minutes. Cook the brown rice at the same time: Sprinkle the rice in a medium saucepan with water, salt and cover for about 20 minutes. cook on a low heat. Take from the fire and another 10 min. to let go.
Arrange the stew over the brown rice and sprinkle with basil.

9.70 Vegetable juice

Promotes digestion, helps to digest fat, supports urination, reduces blood pressure, strengthens immune system, prevents cancer, reduces radiation damage, forcing spleen, is stimulating.
Cooking time approx. 15 min
Calories p. portion: 64
1 portions
Allergens: L

Quantity of ingredients:
Celery root 1/2 oz / 20g. (recommended)
Carrot 1/4 lbs - 4oz / 100g. (recommended)
Tomato 1/4 lbs - 4oz / 100g. (recommended)
Garlic 1 piece / 2g. (yes)
Salt 1 teaspoon / 2g. (little)
Acerola fruit nectar or powder 1/2 teaspoon / 1g. (little)

Cooking instructions:
Peel all ingredients and use the juicer to make a drink. Stir in the acerola.

9.71 Vegetable miso soup with tofu

Very powerful, strengthens after febrile illness, reduces blood pressure, strengthens immune system, prevents cancer, reduces radiation damage, improves blood circulation, strengthens liver and kidney, detoxifying, strengthens the muscles, reduces flatulence, forcing spleen.
Cooking time approx. 15 min
Calories p. portion: 107
4 portions
Allergens: EN

Quantity of ingredients:
Sesame oil 2 table spoons / 35g. (recommended)
Onion (shallot) 1 piece / 20g. (yes)
Carrot 1 piece / 70g. (recommended)
Leek 2 inches / 10g. (yes)
Water 3 cups / 750g. (yes)
Endive salad 2 table spoons / 30g. (yes)
Soy Tofu 2 table spoons / 30g. (yes)
Ginger fresh 1/2 teaspoon / 1g. (yes)
Miso 2 table spoons / 15g. (yes)

Cooking instructions:
In sesame oil first sauté onions, then carrots and a little leek; Pour in water and simmer gently; add the bean sprouts and endive leaves and leave to stand; Tofu cubes, add a little ginger; at the end stir in a little cooled cooking-water the Miso.

9.72 Vegetable semolina soup

Diuretic, harmonizes the stomach and intestines, conducts bowel winds, reduces blood pressure, lowers cholesterol, detoxifying, good to fight loss of appetite, flatulence, inflammatory bowel disease, heartburn, twelffinger intestinal ulcers. Stimulates digestion, reduces pain.
Cooking time approx. 20 min
Calories p. portion: 199
3 portions
Allergens: AEGL

Quantity of ingredients:
Basic recipe for a vegetable soup (nutritious) 2 cup / 500g. (yes)
Potato 1 piece / 80g. (yes)
Parsnip 1 piece / 180g. (yes)
Carrot 1 piece / 120g. (recommended)
Celery root 3/8 lbs - 6oz / 150g. (recommended)
Kohlrabi 1/2 piece / 200g. (recommended)
Beans (green, fresh) 1/4 lbs / 100g. (recommended)
Wheat semolina 2 table spoons / 24g. (yes)
Lovage 1/2 teaspoon / 2g. (yes)
Butter organic 1 table spoon / 20g. (yes)
Soy sauce 1 teaspoon / 3g. (yes)

Cooking instructions:
Worm the prepared vegetable soup; cook the vegetables in the soup softly. Spread some wheatgrass and let it swell. At the end, add lovage-green and a little butter and taste with soy sauce.

9.73 Warming carrot soup

Strengthens and warms, reduces blood pressure, strengthens immune system, prevents cancer, reduces radiation damage, strengthens gastrointestinal function.
Cooking time approx. 30 min
Calories p. portion: 133
3 portions
Allergens: HL

Quantity of ingredients:
Carrot 4 pieces / 250g. (recommended)
Walnut oil 2 table spoons / 20g. (yes)
Onion (shallot) 2 pieces / 40g. (yes)
Anise (Common Fennel) 1/2 teaspoon / 1g. (yes)
Nutmeg 1 pinch / 1g. (yes)
Ginger fresh 1/2 teaspoon / 1g. (yes)
Salt 1 pinch / 1g. (little)
Basic recipe for a vegetable soup (nutritious) 2 cup / 500g. (yes)
Parsley 1 table spoon / 10g. (yes)

Cooking instructions:
Heat walnut oil in a hot pot and fry onions; steam the carrots in it; add anise, nutmeg, a little ginger, salt and sauté everything; add water or vegetable- or meat stock; cook everything soft and then puree; fold in parsley at the end.

Recommendation: Suitable for the cold season, especially if you use meat broth as a liquid for infusion.

9.74 Warming porridge

Strengthens immune system. Diuretic and laxative. Provides vitamin C. Dissolves stones. Promotes digestion, detoxifying, promotes perspiration, reduces blood lipids, stimulates, dissolves stagnation.
Cooking time approx. 10 min
Calories p. portion: 357
1 portions
Allergens: AHO

Quantity of ingredients:
Oat flakes (whole grain) 6 table spoons / 60g. (recommended)
Fig dried 3 pieces / 15g. (yes)
Star anise 1 piece / 1g. (yes)
Ginger fresh 1 pinch / 0,5g. (yes)
Water 1 cup / 120g. (yes)
Maple syrup 1 table spoon / 10g. (little)
Walnuts 1 table spoon (chopped) / 8g. (yes)

Cooking instructions:
Soak the dried fruit. Roast Oatmeal dry. Add dried ginger, star anise or cinnamon, a little grated ginger and boil everything with water to a mash. With maple syrup sweet. Whip grated walnuts and sprinkle before serving.
Caution: Fresh ginger does not drink over a long period of time.

9.75 Wheat fresh grain porridge with pears.

Promotes digestion, supports urination. Affects anorexia, good to fight flatulence, inflammatory bowel disease. Lowers cholesterol, is antiparasitic.
Cooking time approx. 25 min
Calories p. portion: 309
2 portions
Allergens: ANO

Quantity of ingredients:
Wheat 1 cup / 100g. (yes)
Water 2-4 cups / 350g. (yes)
Pear 2 pieces / 300g. (recommended)
Raisins 1 table spoon / 10g. (yes)
Sesame, white 1 table spoon / 8g. (yes)
Sunflower seeds 1 table spoon / 8g. (yes)
Cardamom 1 pinch / 0,3g. (yes)
Salt 1 pinch / 0,3g. (little)

Cooking instructions:
Preparation the night before: Wheat roughly cut; soak overnight.
In the morning: Put the wheat meal with a little hot water; simmer with stirring for about 15 minutes.
Meanwhile, add pear compote, raisins, crushed sesame, sunflower seeds, some ground cardamom, a small pinch of salt.
Variants: with grated apple or seasonal fruit.

9.76 Yellow lentil soup

Strengthens heart and kidney, diuretic, promotes spleen, calms the stomach, promotes digestion, strengthens immune system, prevents cancer, reduces radiation damage, stimulates liver function, antioxidativ.
Cooking time approx. 20 min
Calories p. portion: 155
7 portions
Allergens: A

Quantity of ingredients:
Lentils yellow 1 lbs / 500g. (yes)
Carrot 2 pieces / 150g. (recommended)
Kohlrabi 1 piece / 300g. (recommended)
Onion white 1 piece / 50g. (yes)
Parsley 1/2 bunch / 100g. (yes)
Turmeric (yellow root) 1 pinch / 1g. (recommended)
Cardamom 1 pinch / 1g. (yes)
Salt 1 pinch / 1g. (little)
Olive oil 1 table spoon / 10g. (yes)
Water 4 cup / 1000g. (yes)
Lemon juice 1/2 piece / 15g. (little)
White bread (wheat bread) 7 slices / 140g. (little)

Cooking instructions:
Wash lenses well in a colander. Heat oil in a pot. Add finely chopped onion, sliced carrots, diced kohlrabi and spices, sauté and salt. Add the lentils and cover with water and simmer for 20 minutes. Add water as needed and season with salt. Sprinkle with fresh parsley or fresh green cilantro and drizzle with lemon juice.
Here you can also use red lenses. (same cooking time).
Serve with white bread.

9.77 Yogurt with honey and nuts

Relieves pain, detoxifying, promotes wound healing. Good to fight acute or chronic constipation of the intestine. Dissolves stones.
Cooking time approx. 5 min
Calories p. portion: 258
1 portions
Allergens: GH

Quantity of ingredients:
Yogurt (natural, 3.5% fat) 1/4 lbs - 4oz / 125g. (yes)
Honey 2 table spoons / 30g. (little)
Walnuts 1 table spoon / 12g. (yes)

Cooking instructions:
Mix yoghurt with honey and finely chopped nuts.

10 Effects of food

10.1 Use ingredients: recommendable

Acai powder
Apple (sweet)
Apple puree
Asparagus (green or white)
Beans (green, fresh)
Bearberry leaf
Beer (alcohol-free)
Bitter Herb liqueur
Borage
Broccoli
Brussels sprouts
Carrot
Carrot (Early Carrot)
Carrot juice without sugar
Cauliflower
Celery root
Celery sticks
Chamomile tea
Cherry
Chicory
Chinese cabbage
Cod
Corn germ oil
Cranberries
Cranberry
Cranberry juice
Cream 10% coffee cream
Cream sour 10%
Cream sour 20%
Cucumber
Cucumber (bitter)
Cucumber (spicy cucumber)
Elderberry blossom tee
Fennel
Fish pieces mixed (fresh water)
Fox nut, gorgon nut, makhana
Gourd
Green tea
Herbal tea mix
Herring
Hibiscus
Juniper berry
Kohlrabi
Kudzu
Lamb's lettuce
Lamb's lettuce
Leaf salads (bitter)
Lemon Balm (fresh)
Lentils

Lettuce
Lily bulbs
Linseed oil
Mackerel
Manioc flour
Mediterranean fish (cod, plaice,
haddock, sea eel, mackerel)
Muesli
Noodles (whole grain) with egg
Oat flakes (whole grain)
Oat fusion (baby food)
Peaches
Peaches (canned)
Pear
Peppermint tea
Peppers
Plaice
Plum
Plums
Radicchio
Radish
Radish (white, green, purple-red)
Radish black
Radish horseradish
Rapeseed oil
Red beet
Red cabbage
Rhubarb
Rice (whole grain)
Rice mash
Rice wild (nature rice)
Rosefish
Rucola
Rye wholemeal bread
Salmon
Savory
Savoy cabbage / kale
Sesame oil
Sour cream 15% fat
Sour milk
Soya Cuisine (soy cream)
Soybeans
Stevia (candyleaf, sweetleaf)
Strawberries
Tea mixture uric acid lowering
Tomato
Tomato juice
Trout
Tuna

Turkey breast meat
Turmeric (yellow root)
Turnip
Turnips
Vegetable juice
Watermelon
Wax gourd
Wheat bran
Wheat flour whole grain

Wheat germ oil
Wheat/Rye/Gray-black bread with yeast
White cabbage
Whole grain bread
Wholemeal flour
Wild herbs
Yarrow
Zucchini

10.2 Use ingredients: yes

Adzuki beans
Agar agar (kelp)
Agrimony
Almond
Almond milk
Almond puree
Aloe juice
Amaranth
Amaranth Pops
Anchovy / Sardine
Angelica root
Anise (Common Fennel)
Apple juice (natural cloudy)
Apricot jam
Arrowroot
Artichoke
Aubergine
Avocado
Baking powder
Balm
Bamboo shoots
Banana
Banana (cooking banana)
Banchatee (green tea)
barberry
Barley
Barley flour
Barley grass powder
Barley grouts
Barley malt
Barley not peeled
Basic recipe for a beef soup
Basic recipe for a beef soup (warming)
Basic recipe for a chicken soup
(warming)
Basic recipe for a duck soup
Basic recipe for a fish soup
Basic recipe for a rice soup (Congee)
Basic recipe for a vegetable soup
(nutritious)
Basil
Basil (fresh)

Batavia
Bay leaf
Bean oil
Beef bone marrow
Beef fillet
Beef heart
Beef heart (calf)
Beef lungs (calf)
Beef meat
Beef meat (calf)
Beef meatbones
Beef Oxtail pieces
Beef soup meat
Beef stomach
Beer (alcohol-reduced)
Bitter orange peel
Black beans
Black caraway
Black fungus mushroom
Blackberry dried (unripe fruit)
Blackberry leaves
Black-eyed peas
Blackthorn (Sloe)
Blue mallow tee
Bocksdorn fruits (Fructus Lycii, Goji,
goji berry dried
Boletus mushroom
Borage oil
Boxhorn clover seeds
Brazil nuts
Bread with carob kernel flour
Breadcrumbs (wheat bread, bread roll)
Brie cheese
Broad beans (thick beans)
Buckbean
Buckwheat
Buckwheat (roasted) Kasha
Buckwheat whole grain
Bulgur (cereals)
Burdock root tea
Bush beans
Butter (half fat)

Butter beans white
Butter organic
Buttermilk
Calamari
Camembert
Cantaloupe
Capers in olive oil
Cardamom
Carob flour, St. john's bread
Carp
Cashews
Caviar
Cereal coffee
Chamomile
Champignon
Channa-Dal
Chanterelle
Chard
Chenpi (chinese tangerine bowl)
Chervil
Chervil dried
Chestnut puree
Chestnuts
Chicken Blood
Chicken egg
Chicken egg white
Chicken heart
Chicken meat
Chicken stomach
Chickpeas
Chickweed
Chinese pearl barley
Chives
Chlorella (fresh water)
Chrysanthemum blossom tea
Cinnamon ground
Cinnamon sticks
Clementine
Clove
Cocoa
Coconut flakes
Coconut grated
Coconut meat
Coconut milk
Codfish
Coix (seeds) YiYi Ren
Cola drink (low calorie)
Coriander
Coriander (fresh)
Corn
Corn (fast polenta)
Corn (roasted)
Corn flour
Corn Grease (Polenta)

Corn silk tea
Corn starch
Cottage cheese
Couscous
Cow's milk (1.5% fat)
Cow's milk (whole milk 3.5% fat)
Crab
Cream sour 30%
Creamer
Créme fraiche cheese
Cress
Crispbread
Crucian
Cumin (Caraway seed)
Curcuma
Curd cheese 20%
Curd cheese 40%
Currants (black)
Currants (red)
Daisy
Dandelion (young plants)
Dandelion juice
Dandelionroots tea
Dashi
Dates dried
Dates red
Deer meat
Deer meat
Deer's Bones
Deer's kidneys
Dill
Duck (heart)
Duck (slaughtered)
Ducks egg
Dulse (seaweed)
Dyer's broom herb
Edam cheese
Eel smoked
Emmental cheese
Endive salad
Evening primrose oil
Fennel seeds ground
Fennel tea
Fenugreek (Trigonella foenum-graecum)
Feta cheese
Feta cheese
Fig
Fig dried
Fish sauce
Flounder
Flower pollen
French beans
Fresh cheese

Fresh cheese from soya
Fresh cheese with herbs
Freshwater crab
Freshwater fish
Fructose (glucose)
Gail plum
Galangal
Garam Masala powder
Garlic
Gelatin white
Gelee Royal
Gentian root
Gentian root tea
Ginger fresh
Ginger oil
Ginger powder
Ginkgo fruit
Ginseng
Ginseng root
Goat
Goat and sheep's blood
Goat and sheep's brain
Goat and sheep's milk
Goat and sheep's stomach
Goat cheese
Goose
Goose blood
Goose egg
Goose fat
Goose parts
Gorgonzola
Gouda cheese
Grapefruit dried peel
Grapes red
Grapes white
Grapeseed oil
Grass carp
Green spelt
Ground
Ground caraway
Halibut (Flatfish)
Hawthorn
Hazelnuts
Herbs bitter
Herbs of Provence
Herbs various
Herbs wild
Hibiscus tea
Hijiki
Hokkaido pumpkin
Hop
Horehound leaves
Horse meat
Hyssop

Iceberg lettuce
Jasmine blossoms tee
Jellyfish
Kaki plum
Kalmus
Kefir
Kidney beans (red)
King Solomon's-seal
Kiwi
Kombu seaweed (Saccharina japonica)
Kukicha tea
Kumquats
Ladyfingers
Lamb bones
Lamb meat
Lamb shoulder
Lavender blossoms
Leek
Lemon Balm (dried)
Lemon peel
Lemongrass
Lentils black
Lentils red
Lentils yellow
Licorice root tea
Lima beans
Lime blossom tea
Linseed
Linseed (crushed)
Liver smoothing tea
Lobster
Longane
Loquate / Japanese medlar
Lotus roots
Lotus seeds
Lovage
Lovage seeds
Luo Han Guo fruit
Lychee
Lychee in Preserved
Lye roll
Mallow (Malva sylvestris) blossom tea
Malt
Mango
Mare's milk
Margarine
Marjoram
Mascarpone cheese
Medlar
Millet
Millet flakes
Mineral water
Miso
Miso black (fermented)

Miso paste (soy bean paste)
Mixed Pickles
Mold cheese
Morel (black, dried)
Morel, dried
Mozzarella
Mu Erh Mushroom
Mulberry fruit
Mulled Wine Spice
Mullet
Multi-grain bread (gray bread)
Mung bean
Mung bean sprouting
Mussels
Mustard seeds
Mutton
Mutton
Nasturtium (nose-twister or nose-tweaker)
Nettles
Noodles (wheat) with egg
Noodles (wheat, lasagne) with egg
Noodles (wheat, ribbon noodles) with egg
Noodles (wheat, spaghetti) with egg
Nori, purple seaweed, red algae
Nutmeg
Oat
Oat flakes roasted
Oat flour
Oat meal
Oat milk
Octopus
Octopus
Okra
Olive oil
Olives
Olives green
Onion (shallot)
Onion (spring onion)
Onion read
Onion white
Orange blossom
Orange dried peel
Orange grated peel
Orange peel
Oregano dried
Oregano fresh
Oyster mushroom
Oyster shell powder
Oysters
Palm oil
Papaya
Parmesan

Parsley
Parsley root
Parsnip
Passion blossoms tea
Peanut butter
Peanut oil
Peanuts
Pear juice
Pearl barley
Pearl barley
Peas
Peas, green
Pepper powder (hot)
Pepper white (ground)
Peppermint
Pepperoni
Peppers (rose peppers)
Peppers (sweet)
Peppers powder
Perch
Pheasant
Pickle
Pig blood
Pigeon
Pigeon egg
Pimento
Pine nuts
Pinto beans speckled
Pistachios
Plum dried
Poppy
Pork Bacon
Pork brain
Pork fat (lard)
Pork ham
Pork ham cooked
Pork ham smoked
Pork knuckle
Pork lung
Pork marrow bones
Pork meat
Pork sausage (Bratwurst) Pork skin
Pork stomach
Pork/beef sausage (smoked)
Pork's intestine
Potato
Potato (mealy)
Potato flour
Prickly pear
Processed cheese 12%
processed cheese 30%
Psyllium seed
Pudding powder vanilla
Puff pastry

Pumpernickel (dark bread)
Pumpkin
Pumpkin seed oil
Pumpkin seeds
Quail
Quail egg
Quince
Quinoa
Rabbit
Rabbit (wild)
Rabbit liver
Rabbit meat
Radish leaves
Raisins
Raspberry
Raspberry dried (immature)
Raspberry leaf tea
Reishi mushroom
Ribworttea
Rice (fragrance)
Rice (Gaoliang / Sorghum)
Rice Basmati
Rice black
Rice flour
Rice long grain rice
Rice malt
Rice noodles
Rice red
Rice round grain
Rice starch
Rice sticky
Rice sweet
Rice variety any
Romaine lettuce / lettuce salad
Rose blossom tea
Rose leaf tea
Rosemary
Rusk
Rye
Rye flour
Safflower (Dyer's thistle / Hong Hua)
Saffron
Sage
Sago (cereals)
Salsify
Salt (herbal)
Sea cucumber
Seacrab
Sesame oil roasted
Sesame paste (Tahini)
Sesame, black
Sesame, white
Shark
Sheep's milk

Sheep's milk yoghurt
Shiitake, dried
Shrimp
Shrimps
Skim milk powder
Slug
Sorrel
Sour milk cheese 20%
Sourdough
Soy flour
Soy noodles
Soy sauce
Soy Tofu
Soy Tofu smoked
Soybean milk
Soybean oil
Soybeans, black
Soybeans, blacks, fermented
Soybeans, yellow
Spelled (Dark) bread
Spelled flakes
Spelled grain
Spelled semolina
Spelled wholemeal flour
Spinach
Spiny lobsters
Spurdog (spiny dogfish, Schillerlocken)
St. Benedict's thistle, blessed thistle,
holy thistle, spotted thistle
Star anise
Strawberry jam
Sugar substitute (sweetener)
Sunflower oil
Sunflower seeds
Sweet potato
Tarragon (Estragon)
Thistle oil
Thyme
Thyme dried
Toast bread (whole grain)
Tomato dried
Tomato paste
Tomato puree
Tonic Water
Topinambur
Trout (smoked)
Truffle
Tsampa (roasted barley flour)
Turkey ham
Umeboshi paste
Umeboshi plums (Japanese apricots)
Valerian
Vanilla
Vanilla pod

Vanilla powder
Vanilla sugar natural
Vinegar (Apple vinegar)
Vinegar (Red wine vinegar)
Vinegar Aceto Balsamico
Vinegar Aceto Balsamico white
Wakame
Walnut oil
Walnuts
Walnuts roasted
Water
Water hot
Wheat
Wheat bulgur
Wheat flakes
Wheat flatbread/pita bread
Wheat flour
Wheat semolina

Wheat semolina for children
Wheatgrass juice
Wheatgrass powder
Whey
White beans
Whitefish
Wild boar meat
Wild garlic (garlic spinach)
Wormwood herb
Yam root, yam root tuber
Yarrow tea
Yeast
Yew nut
Yoghurt vanilla
Yogi tea
Yogurt (natural, 1.5% fat)
Yogurt (natural, 3.5% fat)

10.3 Use ingredients: little

Acerola fruit nectar or powder
Agave nectar
Almond marzipan
Apple (sour)
Apricot
Apricot dried
Apricot nectar
Apricots
Apricots juice
Beef kidney
Beef liver
Beer (Pils)
Beer (Top-fermented German dark beer)
Bitter Lemon
Bitter liqueur
Blackberry´s
Blueberry
Blueberry dried
Bread roll
Brown ale
Campari
Carambola (Star fruit)
Cherry (sour)
Chicken liver
Chicken yolk
Chocolate
Chocolate (Diabetic)
Clarified butter
Clementines
Coconut fat
Cranberry

Cranberry jam
Cream (30% fat)
Cream, sweet 30%
Currant (black)
Currant (red)
Currant (white)
Curry
Curry paste red
Eel
Elderberries
Fernet Branca (herbal bitter liqueur)
Fish innards
Fish remains
Ginseng liqueur
Goat and sheep's liver
Gooseberry
Greengage
Guava
Honey
Honey wine (Met)
Lamb kidneys
Lamb liver
Lemon
Lemon juice
Lime
Lychee liqueur
Maple syrup
Margarine (diet)
Martini
Mayonnaise 50%
Mayonnaise 80%
Mirabelle plum

Mustard
Mustard Dijon
Mustard medium hot
Mustard sweet
Nectarine
Orange
Orange jam
Passion fruit
Peanut (roasted)
Pineapple
Pineapple (from a can)
Pineapple juice without sugar
Pork heart
Pork kidneys
Pork Lard
Pork liver
Prosecco
Red berry (without sugar)
Red wine
Rose hip
Rose hip tea
Sake
Salt
Sauerkraut (cutted cabbage fermented)

Sea buckthorn
Sherry (whine)
Sour cherries
Sugar - icing sugar
Sugar brown
Sugar candy white
Sugar cane sugar
Sugar fructose - fruit sugar
Sugar glucose - grapes sugar
Sugar Milk Sugar
Sugar molasses
Sugar palm sugar
Sugar white
Wheat beer
White bread (baguette)
White bread (pretzel sticks)
White bread (roll)
White bread (wheat bread)
White breadcrumbs
White dumpling bread (wheat bread cut into chunks)
White wine
Wild strawberries
Wormwood

10.4 Do not use contra-acting foods

Berries of the season
Berry juice
Black tea
Blackberry jam
Blueberry jam
Blueberry juice
Cherry compote
Cherry juice
Chili (pod or ground)
Coffee
Cola drink
Compote (fruits of the season)
Cooking oil
Currant jam (black)
Currant jam (red)
Currant juice (black)
Fruit mix juice
Fruit tea
Grape juice red

Grape juice white
Grapefruit (Pomelo)
Grapefruit juice
Mango juice
Orange juice
Pepper (ground)
Pepper Cayenne
Peppercorns
Pepperoni, red, pitted, halved
Pepperoni, yellow, pitted, halved
Pomegranate
Raspberry jam
Rum
Spirit
Strawberry Juice
Supplementary nutrition
Tabasco
Tangerine

11 Herbs and their effects

11.1 Bearberry leaf

The ingredients Arbutin, but also the tannins, have an antibacterial effect.

11.2 Basil

It has a beneficial effect on flatulence and nausea, relaxing and soothing. Good to fight emphysema, bronchitis, whooping cough, high blood pressure, headache, mouth odor, warts, hiccup, gout, migraine.

11.3 Mugwort

Reduces bleeding, alleviates pain. In the kitchen, mugwort is used as a spice for fat food. Since it contains many bitter substances, it boosts fat burning and promotes digestion.

11.4 Savory

Stomach-strengthening, soothing and appetizing. Ideal for prevent colds, strengthens the immune system. In case of incontinence or nocturnal wetting (not for children), put the beans in liquor for libido.

11.5 Dill

The medicinal and spice herb has an antispasmodic effect and stimulates gastric juice production. Good to fight flatulence. Antispasmodic for gastrointestinal discomfort.

11.6 Coriander

The essential oils are appetizing, digestive, cramping and soothing in stomach and intestinal disorders.

11.7 Herbs various

Appetizing, lots of trace elements and vitamins

11.8 Cress

Diuretic, supports urination. Good to fight dry mouth, inner agitation, sore throat, diabetes, kidney stones, gastrointestinal complaints, lung problems, menstrual cramps or cancer.

11.9 Chives

Bactericide, prevents cancer, strengthens gastric juice production, promotes digestion and blood circulation, promotes growth, triggers stagnation.

11.10 Lovage

Stimulates digestion, reduces pain. Extracts of the root are used to flush out urinary tract infections and prevent kidney gravel.

11.11 Lily bulbs

Calms nerves, good to fight scaly skin. The onions and the petals are added to ointments in the Orient, which can heal muscles and tendons. White lily (astringent).

11.12 Marjoram

Helps to digest fat foods, strengthens digestive organs, helps to fight colds, strengthens menstruation, promotes skin healing.

11.13 Oregano

It has an anti-digestive, calming and nerve-strengthening effect, helps to fight cramping stomach and intestinal disorders. The ingredient Carvacrol has an anti-inflammatory effect.

11.14 Parsley

Stimulates liver function, detoxifies. Forces urinating. Relieves flatulence. Digestive and menstrual stimulating, birth-accelerating, memory-enhancing, blood-purifying, skin-smoothing.

11.15 Peppermint

Relaxes, frees the lungs and the nose (inhale), regulates the cycle. Stimulates bile flow and bile production, antispasmodic in gastrointestinal disorders, antimicrobial and antiviral.

11.16 Rosemary

Promotes digestion, relieves bloating, strengthens lung, spleen and kidney. Affects the circulation and nerves. Appetizing. Baths help to fight circulatory disorders as well as with gout and rheumatism.

11.17 Sage

Good to fight yeast infections. The leaves have a digestive effect and are used in greasy foods. Antiperspirant effect. Helps to relieve coughing attacks. Dries out (TCM).

11.18 Tea mixture uric acid lowering

Uric acid-lowering.
Mix from the pharmacy or drugstore:
2 parts birch leaves, 1 part of broom, 1 part of stinging nettle, 3 parts of the chopping piece, 1 part of goldenrod.

11.19 Thyme dried

Disinfecting. It stimulates the blood circulation, increases the appetite and helps to digest fat meat better. Strengthens lungs and spleen (TCM).

11.20 King Solomon's-seal

Used to repair wounds or damaged tissue. Good to fight dry cough, earlier also tuberculosis and dysentery, as well as diarrhea and hemorrhoids.

11.21 Yam root, yam root tuber

Solves cramps (in the gastrointestinal tract). Digestive through increased bile production. Anti-inflammatory in rheumatic diseases.
Mucolytic agent for coughing. Relief of menopausal symptoms.

11.22 Lemon Balm (fresh)

Stimulating, antibacterial, encouraging, relaxing, antispasmodic, cooling, antipyretic, analgesic, sweat-inducing, virus-inhibiting. Good for colds, fever, flu, cough, bronchitis, asthma, loss of appetite, bloating, heartburn.

12 Basics of Nutrition

The basic principles of nutrition described herein are general recommendations. They are not aimed at a specific form of therapy. Recommendations concerning a therapy have priority.

12.1 Nutrition

Regular meals in a relaxed atmosphere. A warm breakfast is considered a good start into the day.
The main meals ought to be taken for lunch – supper in the early evening. Pay attention to feeling hungry or sated: don't eat too much nor remain hungry is the rule
Prepare the meals freshly from natural, regional products. Frozen, heat-conserved, industrially prepared or foodstuffs cooked in the microwave oven are rejected.
Choice of foodstuffs according to the season: more cooling food in summer, more warming food in winter.
Eat cooked food at least twice a day. Food and drinks ought to be lukewarm, never ice-cold or hot.
Raw vegetables, briefly cooked vegetables, freshly squeezed juices and mineral water are not recommended. Milk and dairy products are only included in the diet if they don't cause problems.
Don't use therapeutic recipes over a longer period without consulting your doctor or therapist.

Varied food
Enjoy the diversity of foodstuffs. Characteristics of a balanced nutrition are variety, suitable combination and a balanced quantity of rich and low energy foodstuffs (on one hand avoiding undersupply with essential nutrients and on the other hand to take to many undesirable substances).

A lot of Cereal Products - and Potatoes
Bread, pasta, rice, cereal flakes (best wholemeal) as well as potatoes contain almost no fat, but many vitamins, mineral nutrients, trace elements, roughage and secondary plant substances. These foodstuffs ought to be taken with low-fat side dishes.

Vegetables and Fruit – „Take Five" every day ...
5 portions of vegetables and fruit a day, as fresh as possible, briefly cooked, or maybe one portion as a juice – ideal as a side dish to every meal as well as snack between meals: Thus a lot of vitamins, mineral nutrients as well as roughage and secondary plant substances

Daily milk and dairy products
Milk and Dairy Products every Day, once or twice per Week Fish; meat, sausages as well as eggs moderately. These foodstuffs contain valuable nutrients like calcium in the milk, iodine selenium and omega-3 fat acids in saltwater fish. Meat is favorable due to its high content of disposable iron and the vitamins B1, B6 and B12. Quantities of 300 – 600 g meat and sausage per week are sufficient. Prefer low-fat products, especially in meat- and dairy products.

Low-fat and fatty Foodstuffs
Fat supplies us with essential fat acids and fatty foodstuffs contain also fat-soluble vitamins. Fat is high in energy; therefore much fat in the food may cause overweight, possibly also cancer. Too many saturated fat acids may further a tendency for cardio-vascular diseases in the long term. Prefer vegetable oils and fats (e.g. rapeseed-, olive-, soya-oils and solid fats produced therefrom). Beware of invisible fat in meat- and dairy products, pastry and sweets as well as in fast-food and convenience foods. 70 – 90 g fat per day is sufficient.

Moderately Sugar and Salt
Take sugar and foods/drinks containing various kinds of sugar (e.g. glucose syrup) only occasionally. Use herbs and spices as well as a little salt creatively. Prefer salt containing iodine.

Plenty of Liquids
Water is absolutely essential. Drink 1-2 l liquids every day. Prefer water (with or without gas) and other low-calorie drinks. Alcoholic drinks should not be taken.

Tasty Dishes, carefully cooked
Cook the meals with as low temperatures and as short as possible, using little water and fat – this preserves the original taste, keeps the nutrients intact and prevents the production of harmful compounds.

Take time and enjoy the food
Take your Time and enjoy your Food
Eating consciously helps to eat right. The eye enjoys food, too. It's fun, invites to enjoy varied dishes and stimulates the feeling of satiety.

Watch your Weight and stay in Motion
A balanced diet and a lot of exercise and sport (30 – 60 min/day) are a healthy combination. The right weight furthers well-being and health. Thermals, directional effectiveness, digestive power

There are various criteria for judging the effectiveness of herbs and foodstuffs.

The use of certain herbs and ingredients is based on observations of the effects on the body which these foodstuffs, herbs and spices show after having eaten them. The medical science has developed following system: Every ingredient or herb has a directional effectiveness. Furthermore, there are herbs which have a special effect on certain organs.

The basic condition for a healthy metabolism is to obtain sufficient energy from food and that the digestive process doesn't use too much energy. An easily digestible meal makes content and sated, doesn't cause flatulence and fatigue after the meal. The perfect spices increase the healthiness of our meals. Very often, just small doses of herbs and spices will suffice. They are not used to make us sated, but to help our digestive organs to digest the food.

12.2 Recipes

The recipes list the ingredients to be used and the cooking instructions show how the dish is prepared. The list of ingredients shows the concerned quantities as well as the relevance for the therapy. If you find „less than mentioned", try to comply or find an alternative from the „list of recommended foodstuffs". Mostly it shall result just in a small change of taste when you simply avoid this ingredient.

Mild cooking methods: boiling, stewing, poaching, steaming
Strong cooking methods: barbecuing, roasting, frying, smoking
Balanced cooking methods: deep-frying, baking brick
Deep-freezing and warming in the microwave oven should be avoided (denaturalization).

12.3 Foodstuffs

Foodstuffs have an effect on body and soul like medicinal herbs, only a very much milder one. Dietary advice is mainly based on regional foodstuffs. The knowledge about the effects of each foodstuff and the knowledge, when which foodstuff shall be used, is based on the orthodoschool of medicine. Use ecologic-organic products, if possible. As everything should be cooked for a long time due to a better digestability and very rarely eaten raw, the food agrees with everyone.

The classification of the foodstuffs according to their effect on the body is the basis in order to achieve a harmonious status of health.

Dietary advisors do not recommend certain foodstuffs for everyone. The individual diet is tailor-made for the individual constitution.

Buy only fresh and ripe fruit and vegetables. You ought to leave unripe fruit and vegetables and such with brown spots and wilted leaves behind in the market. In this case take deep-frozen goods (never ready-to-serve dishes!). Fruit and vegetables are deep-frozen immediately after harvesting and often contain more vitamins and minerals than the goods from the vegetable shelf. Whereas conserved or tinned goods contain very much less biological substances. Also, salt, sugar and others are mostly added to the latter. Never leave the foodstuffs in the water after washing them to avoid that many vital substances get drowned. Clean salads, fruit and vegetables immediately before serving.

Please make sure of the hygienic processing of foodstuffs. Clean your salads, fruit and vegetables carefully. When cooking with meat, prepare all ingredients first and then process the meat products. Clean the worktop and tools very carefully. Wooden surfaces ought to be treated with a mild disinfectant regularly in order to reduce germination.

Store fruit and vegetables separately, if possible. Harvested fruit and vegetables are still alive and emit e.g. ethylene gas, which makes other products ripen and age faster. Keep meat and fish in the closed packaging or store them in the fridge in closed containers.

12.4 Herbs

There are some basic rules for storing medicinal herbs. On principle, herbs must be protected from direct sunlight, humidity and heat.

Containers for the storage of herbs may be glasses, ceramic jars and even plastic containers. However, plastic is a rather unsuitable material and should only be a short-term solution. In case of glass containers, use a dark material.

Medicinal herbs cannot be kept for any long period. The shelf life of herbs is limited. However, it can be prolonged with suitable storage. The place should be dark, rather cool and absolutely dry. A wooden medicine cabinet, placed not directly next to a source of heat, would be ideal. Never buy large quantities of herbs so as not to have to throw them away. Label the container with the name of the herb and the date of harvesting or processing.

13 Other dietic-books

The following syndromes of dietetics, TCM or for a therapy supplement for cancer are available.

Dietetics

E001. Nutrition of the infant - baby food
E002. Nutrition during lactation
E003. Nutrition in old age
E004. Nutrition of children and adolescents
E005. Nutrition of athletes
E006. Light weight
E007. Pregnancy
E008. Full food

Protein and electrolyte - kidneys
E009. (hemodialysis) dialysis treatment
E010. Acute renal failure
E011. Chronic renal insufficiency
E012. Nephrotic syndrome
E013. Kidney stones (nephrolithiasis)

Gastrointestinal tract - pancreas
E014. Acute pancreatitis (inflammation of the pancreas)
E015. Chronic pancreatitis (inflammation of the pancreas)

Gastrointestinal tract - small intestine and large intestine
E016. Acute obstipation (constipation)
E017. Chronic obstipation (constipation)
E018. Colon irritabile
E019. Diverticulitis
E020. Acquired lactose intolerance (lactose malabsorption)
E021. Fructose malabsorption
E022. Glutensensitive enteropathy (celiac disease)
E023. Colectomy
E024. Short Bowel Syndrome

Gastrointestinal tract - liver, gallbladder, bile ducts
E025. Acute and chronic hepatitis (inflammation of the liver)
E026. Cholelithiasis (bile stones)
E027. fatty liver
E028. cirrhosis

Gastrointestinal tract - Stomach and duodenal intestine
E029. Acute gastritis
E030. Chronic gastritis
E031. Stomach bleeding
E032. Ulcus ventriculi and duodenal ulcer
E033. Condition after gastric surgery

Gastrointestinal tract - oral cavity and esophagus
E034. Stomatitis
E035. Esophageal carcinoma (esophageal cancer)
E036. Refluosophagitis (heartburn)

Special diseases
E037. Phenylketonuria (PKU)
E038. Rheumatic joint diseases

Metabolism
E039. Obesity (overweight)
E040. Diabetes mellitus
E041. Eating disorders (underweight)

Fat metabolism
E042. Hypercholesterolaemia (increased cholesterol level)
E043. Hepatic Encephalopathy

Heart and circulation
E044. Arteriosclerosis (arterial calcification)
E045. Heart insufficiency
E046. Hypertension
E047. Hyperuricaemia and gout

Changed nutrient requirements
E048. In case of fever
E049. For malignant diseases
E050. After burns
E051. Radiation and chemotherapy

CANCER
E100. Pancreatic cancer
E101. Bladder cancer
E102. Blood cancer (leukemia)
E103. Breast cancer
E104. Colorectal cancer
E105. Gastric cancer
E106. Kidney cancer
E107. Esophageal cancer

TCM
E200. Bladder - moisture heat in the bladder
E201. Bladder - moisture and cold in the bladder
E202. Bladder - emptiness and cold in the bladder
E203. Large intestine - external cold affects the large intestine
E204. Large intestine - moisture heat in the large intestine
E205. Large intestine - heat blocks the intestine II acute
E206. Large intestine - dryness of the colon
E207. Large intestine - Yang deficiency (cold)
E208. Heart - Blood insufficiency
E209. Heart - Blood stagnation
E210. Heart - Fire
E211. Heart - Hot mucus clogs the heart pores

E212. Heart - Cold mucus clogs the heart pores
E213. Heart - Qi deficiency
E214. Heart - Yang deficiency
E215. Heart - Yin deficiency
E216. Liver - Ascending Liver Yang
E217. Liver - Blood deficiency
E218. Liver - Blood stagnation
E219. Liver - Moisture heat in liver and gall bladder
E220. Liver - Fire
E221. Liver - Gall bladder Qi-Empty
E222. Liver - Cold in the liver meridian
E223. Liver - Qi stagnation
E224. Liver - Wind
E225. Liver - Wind with ascending liver Yang
E226. Liver - Wind with blood anemic
E227. Liver - Wind with extreme heat
E228. Lung - Qi deficiency
E229. Lung - Mucus-moisture in the lungs
E230. Lung - Mucus-heat in the lungs
E231. Lung - Mucus-cold in the lungs
E232. Lung - Dryness of the lungs
E233. Lung - Wind-heat attacks the lungs
E234. Lung - Wind-cold affects the lungs
E235. Lung - Yin deficiency
E236. Stomach - Bloodstagnation
E237. Stomach - Fire
E238. Stomach - Cold with liquid
E239. Stomach - Nutrition stagnation
E240. Stomach - Qi deficiency
E241. Stomach - Rebellious Qi
E242. Stomach - Yin Emptiness
E243. Spleen - Heat and moisture attack the spleen
E244. Spleen - Coldness and moisture affects the spleen
E245. Spleen - Qi deficiency
E246. Spleen - Qi deficiency + Declining spleen Qi
E247. Spleen - Qi deficiency + spleen does not control the blood
E248. Spleen - Yang deficiency
E249. Kidney - Heart and kidney no longer communicate
E250. Kidney - Jing deficiency
E251. Kidney - Kidneys cannot receive the Qi
E252. Kidney - Qi is not stable
E253. Kidney - Yang deficiency
E254. Kidney - Yin deficiency

For further information visit di-book.com.